HIMPRESSIONS:

The Blackwoman's

guide to
Pampering
The Blackman

A MANUAL

---

by Valerie B. Shaw, M.PR

Published by:
Turn The Page Productions
Glendale, CA 91205

5 6 7 8 9 10

ISBN: 09638121-9-X

Cover, Book Design & Typesetting by Ellison / Goodreau

Printed & Distributed by:
D & J Publications, Inc.
229-21B Merrick Blvd.
Laurelton, N.Y. 11413

For Mother, Hoppie, "Doc" Smith
and other angels I have known.

Pleasant words are as a honeycomb,
Sweet to the soul, and health to the bones.

-Proverbs 16:24-

CONTENTS

Personal Acknowledgments & Author's Notes .... **vii**
About the Author .... **ix**
Dedication .... **xi**

Foreword **3**

1. Himpressions: Where They Come From **13**
2. Insecurity: The Black Plague of Relationships **19**
   Eleven Personal Keys to Slaying
   The Beast of Insecurity **26**
3. The 4-1-1 On Attracting Attention:
   A How To & Where To Primer **29**
4. Picking & Choosing or One Woman's Hash
   Is Another's Gourmet Feast **41**
5. "Nice" **51**
6. If You Were A...The Man Behind the Mask............... **57**
7. Beware The FAAWABA! **63**
8. Condomphobia & Intimacy In The AIDS Generation ... **73**
   50 Ways To Say No To Sex **81**
9. 101 Ways To Pamper Your Blackman **85**
10. The Kitchen Is Open But There's No Free Lunch **91**
11. Loss & The Loving Void **99**
12. Goodbye. . . Goodbye. . . Goodbye Again:
    When It's Time To Leave **107**

Afterword **117**
Himpression Nuggets **119**

PERSONAL ACKNOWLEDGMENTS
AND AUTHOR'S NOTES

This slender manual, which is extracted from a considerably larger volume, is dedicated to Love and to all of those who have allowed me to share it:

To the crew of master craftsmen at the Shoe Healer, the "Cowboys," who cheered this *Guide* from the day of its inception.

And to the patrons, the gentlemen and gentle ladies so eager to share their questions and experiences—all in the hope of discovering or nurturing healing relationships.

From long ago, thanks to my earliest role models—Jo Bonita Perez, the first nice girl I ever knew and Johnny Simmons, the first nice guy.

This work in progress is dedicated to my former husbands and lovers who taught me the rules, and to my beloved family and friends who threw out the rule book.

To my current personal and professional mentors, coaches and guides—in particular Earline and Bill Johnson, Richard Robinson, Dwan Smith-Fortier, Elvin Ricks, Benita Shaw Lewis, Bennie Shaw, Antolina and Rodney Connor, Donna Mungen, Stephanie Ardrey, Mary Margaret Swift and Cristina Najera—to whom I owe much of my spiritual growth, mental health and well-being. Thanks for keeping me grounded.

To my friend Warren Lanier, Sr., who has taken his professional interest in me extremely personally, thank you.

Further, to Brother Khalifa Abdur-Raheem, I give special acknowledgment and praise for serving as the senior advisor on my theories, the senior editor on the work and my spiritual guide throughout my quest for faith and grace.

Other editors I wish to thank are Antoina Connor and Candice Wilson. And Robert Epstein, my first editor.

A special thanks to Candice Wilson who has accepted me as her adopted mother, loving me in all my humanity.

And to my son, Andrew, the purest love I shall ever know, this book is for you.

As ever and as always I thank God for allowing my words to be a conduit for understanding between all people. Through His tender mercy I have accepted my mission as a writer and as a woman and thank Him for allowing me to speak.

᏶ Valerie B. Shaw was the first African-American wo-man to own a chain of state-of-the-art retail shoe re-pair and shine salons in the United States. From her Hollywood base—on the world-famous corner of Sun-set and Vine—and beyond, she became known as the "First Lady of Soles."

She is a former feature writer for the *Los Angeles Times* and a national award-winning business writer who holds a master's degree in Public Relations from the University of Southern California.

She is a Black film historian, producer of the *Black Hollywood Yesterday* series of calendars and memorabilia.

She is a business leader, sitting on the Board of Di-rectors of the Hollywood Chamber of Commerce; a television personality, with appearances on several talk shows including the "Sally Jesse Raphael Show", "The Montel Williams Show" and "The Love Connection"; lecturer; mentor and community activist who is the co-founder of the Black Journalists' Association of Southern California.

So much for the stats.

Valerie B. Shaw is a Libra lady who is forever in love with Love. At 48, Valerie Shaw is the single mother of a seven-year-old son and is in between marriages.

Far from being jaundiced by divorce, she believes in men, marriage and monogamy.

Valerie Shaw admits that she is neither wise nor witty by nature. She finds in writing, however, both wit and wisdom in the idiosyncrasies of Love.

Himpressions: The Blackwoman's Guide To Pampering The Blackman is a compilation of observations on, and experiences in, relationships accumulated over the past 30 years.

Her goal, as a Black woman, parent, journalist, business leader and community activist, is to help Black men and women—Brothers and Sisters—find joy in each other's company appreciating their similarities and respecting their differences.

DEDICATION

To men, all men,
Your passion's deep.
If only passion's not put to sleep.
To women, my Sisters,
Who know not their power,
This is the time
Now is the hour.
Heal the wounds
Of a past out of control,
Today, the present, is ours to hold.
Oh mothers, daughters,
Sisters, wives and friends,
Let go the anger,
Let us celebrate our men.

—Valerie B. Shaw—

HIMPRESSIONS:

The Blackwoman's
guide to
Pampering
The Blackman

___

A MANUAL

If you are concerned about the effect your presence has on others, you care about the impression you are making.

There are first impressions, lasting impressions, good impressions and wrong impressions. But those, it seems to me, fall short of describing the impressions we have about [and try to leave with] the opposite sex.

Women, in particular, are concerned about the impression they make on men. Did I say concerned? I mean *consumed*.

It is no secret that men are our favorite topic of conversation at work, over lunch, on the telephone and behind their backs. It is amazing how much time we spend dissecting a male's behavior and peccadillos.

From the books we read to the shows we watch, from where we go to what we wear, men are our oxygen.

For every one man's action there is a shower of female reaction. We always have something to say. Or to add.

A date that took three hours to enjoy, takes six hours to dissect. After describing the event in more detail than CNN covering the Gulf War, you ask your girlfriend, "Does it sound like he likes me?"

As if she occupied the press box in the back seat of his car, you press on. "Do you think he'll ask me out again?"

If she is a truly wise friend she'll admit that she doesn't know. But that's not what you want to hear. That's not why you called her! Girlfriend is supposed to wrap up your story, like Oprah, and the audience will applaud.

[Cut to the commercial.]

You want some assurances. Hope. Some kind of guarantee that he's thinking about you as much as you're thinking about him.

Now, things are bad between the sexes all over the world. Divorce rates are soaring among all races. Unhappiness and loneliness are epidemic.

Feelings of isolation, today, are as universal as mother's milk. However, somewhere between Vietnam and the Justice Clarence Thomas confirmation hearings, Black women have been especially hard hit by shrapnel from the War Between the Sexes.

In Vietnam we lost over 30,000 of our brightest and finest young men. That was the '60s, when life was supposed to be simple.

Then along came the '70s and '80s. Sisters lost about two generations of Brothers [or, a couple of million men] to drugs, crime and homosexuality and their deadly cousins—homicide, prison and AIDS.

Many of us, shaken into the '80s reality of scarcity, went back to school to get a degree or to advance our education. Many of us climbed the career ladder—just as we expected him to do.

While that was a personally satisfying trip in the '80s, doesn't it piss you off [just a teeny bit] that when you look back—from the '90s—most Brothers are no-where to be found?

Some unfortunate Sisters slid backwards—moved home or into the lap of Big Brother Welfare along with their growing families.

By now, in the '90s, Sisters sadly admit that we are the biggest casualties in the Sexual Revolution.

Sisters today are used to operating their lives with-out a man at the helm. So, when we do meet the real "endangered" Blackman, who has his act together, we are so used to being in the drivers' seat that we refuse to give up the wheel.

["He doesn't know where he's going. Give me that steering wheel!" CRASH!!!]

It is the same independence which frees us to be the heads of our families that makes us the butts of the Blackman's jokes.

We are sarcastic Sapphires (reminiscent of "Amos 'n' Andy's" Sapphire, the shrilling shrew married to the Kingfish).

We are demanding Delilahs who won't just give a Brother a haircut. Brothers say we're trying to cut off their balls too.

While she stood tall as a card-carrying heroine to most Sisters, Anita Hill simply confirmed to many Brothers that it's open season on the Blackman.

"The Sisters' Revenge," one of my male patrons cried, following the Supreme Court confirmation face-off between Anita Hill and Clarence Thomas and the rape trial of Mike Tyson. "Women today will stop at nothing to ruin us."

Now, not only do our men face incredible obstacles on the job and in the street, but they say that Sisters are taking our private grievances with Brothers to the airwaves.

🐚   🐚   🐚

Without assigning blame, I'd just like to point out that somewhere between buying into the stereotypes and selling our men out, Black women have fashioned for themselves a manless matriarchy.

The Brother doesn't have a chance.

Experience has taught us that if a Brother doesn't suffer from cold feet or spinelessness, he's got a case of "Jungle Fever."

He's going to take you for a ride or you're going to get soaked. Before he steals your heart, you might as well cut him off at the knees.

We reserve these judgments strictly for the Black-man, I'm afraid.

You won't hear too many mothers warning their daughters about the perils of falling for a White man—Jew or Gentile. And we're altogether mute on Hispanic and Asian men. But *don't* we have a lot to say about our Brothers?

I call our radical and emotionally-charged opinions about the Blackman *Himpressions* because our feelings go way beyond mere impressions.

Our *Himpressions* of Brothers are the result of generations of estrangement. [We haven't really spoken civilly to each other since Slavery, when we had only one common oppressor.]

"He's lazy."

"That womanizer. He's no damned good."

"... And he'll never amount to nothin'. That sorry s.o.b."

Those are our *Himpressions* of Black men in the '90s.

Forgetting that our men are also our sons, the result of our negative *himpressions* is the generational dysfunctional African-American family, which is as common today as divorce and welfare.

Come on, Girlfriend, admit it. We do have a problem.

❦   ❦   ❦

I'm a woman. A Blackwoman. But I'm also a writer, who working in a male-dominated business, observed both points of view. Over half of my customers and all of my "Cowboys" [that's what I call my master cobblers and shine personnel] were men.

From what I hear—from hundreds of men and the Cowboys—is that Brothers are frustrated with Sisters in a major way.

"That nagging bitch makes me want to stay in the streets," says one customer, a hard-working self-employed single father.

"What does the broad want?," another flails his arms in the air with all the anger, frustration and disappointment he has pent up inside.

"Just tell her I'm not here," shouts one of the Cowboys. "That woman must not have anything to do except bug me since Oprah's over," he mutters.

I wondered how many times had I been the topic of a juicy barber shop or shoe shine parlor conversation?

[Oh well, other men, other times.]

The frustration with Sisters seems to be a common thread that runs through the very fabric of the Brotherhood. To them we are all alike.

Now where have I heard *that one* before?

I am amazed at all the years I wasted on trying to understand the Blackman. With all the time my girlfriends and I have dedicated to dissecting the African-American male psyche we could have retired the national debt or discovered the cure for AIDS.

So much time. So much wasted time. So much energy. So much wasted energy!

'So STOP,' I said to myself after eavesdropping on one particularly frank all-male conversation between four old friends catching up on old times.

'Stop trying to figure out what a Black man thinks. Ask him'.

Brothers are, almost always, willing to talk about their feelings, their preferences, what makes them happy and what gets on their last nerve.

Most Brothers wonder why it's taking us so long to ask.

It occurred to me that if we understood what Brothers think—changing our *Himpressions*—we could save ourselves a lot of needless grief and help to create healthy relationships between Black men and women in the process.

❦   ❦   ❦

So what do we do with this understanding?

"I'm just looking for a woman who will pamper me," said one of my very handsome bachelor friends.

PAMPER?!

What an interesting choice of words.

Pamper as in coddle? Overindulge? Give in to? Kiss up to?

Pamper. That old notion that must have come out of the charcoal ages of the Antebellum South.

Pamper. That's what the man said.

I had to think about that one for a moment.

You pamper a baby or a household pet don't you? You also pamper the people you love.

As with an abused puppy or neglected child, you must necessarily give a little more love, a little more understanding and a lot of compassion to make the relationship work. The time and effort you expend is—in a word—*pampering.*

Well, by everyone's acknowledgment—social scientists, the media, the clergy, and the bookie on the corner—the Blackman is both neglected and abused. And if that's not enough, the Blackman in the 1990's is the most endangered species walking on two legs on the North American continent.

Hum-m-m, abused, neglected and endangered. It sounds to me like Brothers deserve some pampering.

Today, as we measure our lives in nanoseconds, survival issues pressing in like ants on a watermelon, *pampering* takes on new meaning.

In the past two years I've asked hundreds of men to comment on the notion of *pampering.*

One pampered Blackman I know described his soulmate as a woman who provided a refuge from his stress. "She *knows* how to pamper me, man," he said with a quarter moon grin lighting his face. "My lady makes me smile, keeps me laughing and reminds me every day that she's in my corner."

"I'd feel pampered if I could find a woman who wanted to help me make some money instead of plotting to take my money," said one of my bachelor customers.

"All she needs to do is rub my back and keep my feet warm," quipped another.

The word *pamper* had raised a torrent of response.

In most cases, among the less verbose Brothers,

pampering meant just being nice. Kind. Understanding. A woman who wouldn't take them for an emotion-filled ride on a run-away train, headed straight for the brick wall side of the poor house.

Pampering a man was just that simple.

And that was the genesis of this *Guide.*

As a social scientist I've got to tell you that developing a model of understanding between hassled Brothers and hostile Sisters is a great research challenge.

[It might be easier to stop the genocide in Somalia.]

Amazingly, in the 24-months I spent compiling and testing these new *Himpressions,* I discovered more fine, eligible Brothers, hungry for meaningful relationships than I had in the previous 24-years.

Brothers were everywhere! Suddenly I was holding seven winning numbers in the Lottery of Love.

So here I am, three husbands, several lovers, and an ocean of heartache later, enjoying new waves of Brothers washing onto my shores.

I've met dozens of other Sisters—age, looks nor social status withstanding—who have also found an abundance of manna in the wasteland. These are Sisters who have more dates than a homemade fruitcake.

Their secret?

Well, that's what *Himpressions* is all about.

Don't tell me there are no good Black men. That's like saying there are no good apples on the old apple tree.

I am convinced that many Sisters are either picking fruit in the wrong orchard or trying to harvest a crop out of season. [Whatever.]

I just think that it's time for Sisters to dig in and take the initiative in harvesting a bumper crop of men. Today, in the '90s, isn't it time to replant our relationships in fertile soil?

Admittedly, *Himpressions* is not for everyone. If you are looking for something high-tech or high-sounding, you are turning the wrong page. There is absolutely nothing complex about this *Guide*.

Himpressions: The Blackwoman's Guide To Pampering The Blackman is a recipe book of "beauty shop" secrets harvested in a Hollywood shoe shine parlor and beyond, that may help my Sisters to serve our starving Brotherhood a slice of fresh, warm apple pie in the waning years of this millennium.

Now let's get busy!

CHAPTER 1

HIMPRESSIONS: WHERE THEY COME FROM

To my late maternal grandmother—growing up in the rural Jim Crow South, assaulted and abused by field bosses, workers, husbands and boyfriends alike—all men were dogs.

That's the sermon she preached to her dying day.

Of all my relatives, on both sides of the family, and of all my friends, I can count only a handful or two of *successfully* married couples. Successful, as in working together for common goals and truly caring for each other's well-being.

Most Black folks I know are in dysfunctional relationships. Or abusive relationships.

Aside from the clinically dysfunctional, many a Sister is the primary bread-winner, chief care-giver and sole decision-maker in her family. This leads to a very unhealthy role reversal, as the Sister considers it a part of her job to keep her spouse in his place—somewhere behind her, along with the kids. After all, she's the one doing the moving and shaking. Everyone else is just baggage. [Or, along for the ride.]

❧   ❧   ❧

Don't you wonder where we get our *himpressions* about Black men from?

From our grandmothers, half of whom raised their children (our mothers and fathers) without a man; or from our mothers, two-thirds of whom became jaundiced by abandonment, loneliness and non-payment of child support?

Or do we get these one-dimensional *himpressions* about Brothers from our friends; who are more often than not, single or divorced, bitter and alone?

From television? The movies? Music? Maybe from "Lifestyles Of the Rich and Famous?" "Def Comedy Jam?" "Martin?" The soap operas? Or Jockey shorts commercials?

The answer, sadly, is all of the above. Much of our information about men comes second-hand, it's hearsay or it's from the media.

Most Sisters out there in the male marketplace were raised by single mothers. What are those statistics? I've read that 68% of all Black households are headed by women.

Personally, I don't know of more than a couple of dozen households that aren't now or haven't, for long stretches of time, been headed by women.

I wonder how we can form a healthy respect for men when most Sisters don't even know the opposite sex? Most of us Sisters were raised by our mothers!

So where was your father during your formative

years?

My dad was in a new marriage, raising another family—completely uninvolved in my sister's and my upbringing. Some fathers were deceased. Others were in jail or in the military.

Same thing. They were gone!

Even those of us who shared growing up with brothers, were, more often than not, estranged from male siblings. While our brothers practiced their manhood thing—identifying with absent fathers or ever-present friends—sisters were rarely brought into the inner circle. Our observations about men were developed at the dinner table or from fights over use of the bathroom.

I don't know too many adult Black siblings—brothers and sisters—who are close. In fact, I don't know too many Black men and women, of any relation, who are tight.

ॐ　　ॐ　　ॐ

It's a strange war we're waging against each other. Both Sisters and Brothers admit that we share the same struggle to survive in these troubling times. We don't have a problem admitting, anyway, that we do need each other on many fronts.

Take the money thing. Rent (or that hefty mortgage), car maintenance, the ever-rising cost-of-living and double-digit inflation. The truth is, two do live cheaper than one.

And with AIDS overtaking even greater numbers of African-Americans than the general population; two, these days, also live *healthier* than one.

Ask the opposing sides: both armies say they want peace.

Both the Brothers and the Sisters say they want to come together.

I hear it everyday: "Girl, can't you introduce me to a good man?" one Sister begs her friend.

"When I do," says her friend, "it'll be as my husband."

From the other side of the war zone I hear, "Man, I'd be married tomorrow if I could find a woman who wanted more from me than help with rent and babysitting."

The blame, says each side, rests squarely with the other gender.

Girlfriend says, "You know, there just aren't any good men who aren't married."

Homeboy, on the other hand, declares, "Man, I'd give anything to meet a woman who was down for me."

Meanwhile the "personals" are bulging. The bars are bursting.

Everybody's looking.

A Brother will spend $200 for a night of cruzin' and catching and the next morning have nothing more than a headache, some empty bottles and one spent condom between the sheets.

A Sister will spend two hours primping for a date she really doesn't even want to go on.

Both the Brothers and the Sisters are looking for the best, but fully expecting to find the worst.

❦   ❦   ❦

Low expectations bring poor results.

Many of my Sisters get just what they expect.

It seems to me that the Blackwoman's struggle to meet and keep the endangered Blackman in her pocket is like going to Las Vegas with an empty purse and bad credit.

With no money, she can't even play the slot machine.

And if you can't play, you sure can't win.

What's happening?

Building positive relationships out of negative perceptions is a lot like building sand castles at the beach. Oh, what a big wave will do to a fragile sand castle.

If the old *himpressions* aren't working, why don't we form some new ones? Maybe by changing our perceptions and *himpressions* about the Blackman we can bring about a positive change in our relationships with him.

Let me warn you though, my Sister, by throwing out all of your tired, old *himpressions* about the Blackman, making your mind up to build new ones, you will, at first, recognize a tremendous void in your conversations with your girlfriends.

Suddenly, without anything negative to say about Brothers, you'll have nothing to talk about.

But if your goal is to build positive, lasting relationships with our Brothers, I promise you that unless you abandon that old mine shaft of past hurts and rejections, you'll never strike gold.

Just look at it this way: It's impossible to strike gold in a deserted mine shaft. It's already been worked over.

Let's start fresh as squeezed orange juice.

Throw out those tired old experiences with the evening trash and start anew.

For goodness sake—and for your happiness sake—don't take my word on it. I invite you to form some new *himpressions* of your own.

CHAPTER 2

INSECURITY:
THE BLACK PLAGUE OF RELATIONSHIPS

ॐ The way I see it, the Black Plague of our species is *Insecurity*. To know how to be good to someone, you've got to learn to be good to yourself, first!

So, the first step in pampering your man is really learning to pamper yourself. That means shedding the winter coat of insecurity and walking, bikini-confident into the sunshine.

Don't even think that you can't do it!

If I could, anyone can.

For most of my life I've felt like an outsider—an uninvited guest at Christmas dinner; a dwarf playing guard in the NBA; a pimply-faced pubescent modeling on a Paris runway.

I can still recall the horrors of my teenage years. When I danced with a boy I had sweaty palms, knocking knees and my body gave off that funky smell of fear and iminent danger.

Needless to say, I didn't dance much. But to compensate, I learned to talk. And talk. And talk.

That, I was good at.

They say that women generally talk too much.

I recall one guy I had set my sights on telling me that I'd be great if I didn't try so hard to be great.

I had no idea what he meant. I just kept on talking. I could be counted on, in those days, to monopolize any conversation.

I could have taken the gold medal in the Talk Olympics.

That's before I got in the shoe shine business.

Believe it or not, more progressive men over the age of 25 get their shoes shined than step into any locker room.

Just ask a Brother. A successful man knows that his appearance counts from head to toe. It's a grooming thing.

See, the shoe shine parlor is the male equivalent of the female beauty shop. Just like us—getting a scalp massage during a shampoo—men getting their feet worked on feel relaxed. And comfortable.

And they talk, just like Sisters. Oh, do Brothers love to talk!

Sometimes at work I felt as though I was eavesdropping on a party line. Or listening at the bedroom door of a bachelor party.

Needless to say, I had more fun on my job than a pig in a garbage dump or a fox in the hen house. I've heard more secret yearnings and confessions from my Brothers than Dear Abby.

'That's interesting,' I observed one day. 'I'm learning more about men by listening than I ever did by talking.'

I think now that most people—women especially—talk incessantly out of insecurity. We're uncomfortable with silence or we want to impress a man with how many virtues we possess.

God, if we leave something out he won't recognize how sensitive and intelligent we are. Better get it all in—in one breath!

Have you ever noticed at the end of an evening how much of your life's tragedy you've shared but how little you know about him?

He might know your net worth and you don't even know his phone number.

So you want to be different in his eyes? Well, surprise, my Sister, if you're talking enough to get dry-mouth, you fit his stereotype. You are as common as a potato in a sack.

Listen! It's as easy as that.

Once you warm up to the idea of listening you'll be amazed at how your own insecurity will dissipate.

You're not alone on this planet.

Lots of people feel the same way you do. They face fears, challenges, disappointments just like you do.

The more you begin to experience empathy for other people, the less insecure you will feel within yourself.

The good habit of listening leads to learning—about yourself, about him, about other points of view.

And with two of every three Black marriages ending in divorce, I think it's time for someone to do some listening.

❦   ❦   ❦

If talking too much or listening too little is not the problem, many Sisters are driven deep into the clutches of *Insecurity* by an abusive mate.

If you're being used as a door mat, pillow or punching bag, it is no wonder that you feel like you're less than the furniture.

If you are too mauled to get a grip on your own survival, then of course you are too insecure to leave.

In far too many cases, Sisters choose to stay in an unhappy relationship. More than that, they stretch it out.

"What did I do wrong?"

"What can I do to make him love me?"

"What will I do with the rest of my life without him?"

I asked myself that question a thousand times over the years. Through two of my three marriages, divorces and a number of other doomed relationships.

I recall hibernating for three years following the break up of my engagement to a prominent local physician. And another two years over the dissolution of my second marriage.

Five years of my life were lost to the feeling that I could not live without a man to love me.

One thing I think Brothers learn in sports, but Sisters don't learn anywhere, is that getting dumped is not personal.

In every contest—as in sports, as in the military, in business and the War Between the Sexes—there is a winner and there is a loser. A dumper and a dumpee. It's not personal. Someone's just got to bite the dust.

Looking at it that way, Girlfriend, if you spend all your time mourning lost loves, I guarantee that you'll feel sorry for yourself. And self-pity is the life blood of *Insecurity*.

Self-pity will blind you to your potential and overshadow all of your accomplishments. It will rob you of the pleasure of all future relationships. And you'll be far too busy feeling sorry for yourself today to build a more promising tomorrow.

In moments when I begin to feel self-pity, I remind myself that life is not a hotel. You can't just lay there and expect to be served. You've got to get up.

Getting up means moving. And, as you move through life, the scenery changes.

I mean, if the only people you know now are the same people you've always known, you won't have any room to meet the people you haven't met yet.

Right?

Your best friend in the first grade is probably not your best friend today. Different times bring different folks into your life.

There! I rest my case.

Okay, so developing a strong sense of self-esteem isn't as easy as cracking open an egg.

The good feelings we have about ourselves are often buried beneath layers of social and personal heartache, rejection and neglect. But the good feelings are there, somewhere.

Every now and then—when you get your hair done in a sexy new style, lose weight, get an unexpected compliment from your boss or make a positive decision—you feel the rush of self-esteem.

That rush reminds you of all the self-confidence that is your potential. For just a moment you are Queen of the Universe.

Now, what if you hadn't made the move to get the hairdo, lose the weight, put in the work that led to the compliment or make the decision in the first place?

It was you—after all—who took control of your destiny. If only for a minute you took the risk; and you reaped the reward.

Now, if you'll admit that you had the power over that single moment, it must also hold true that you have the power over every moment. [Every moment, after all, is just a single moment.]

See, it's as easy as that. You're in control.

When you stop taking your losses with Brothers so personally you'll discover that Love is its own reward. You can count yourself lucky if you still have the capacity to fall in love. Some people have been so mauled in relationships they have no love to give.

"Put that love out there enough and it will boomerang back to you," says one Sister who became engaged to her Mr. Wonderful a few months ago.

A secure and confident Sister is not afraid to love; she just knows when to stop. She doesn't have spare time for pining or whining about what she doesn't have or who she is not with.

When you are involved in life, you are too busy getting out there to be shackled by *Insecurity*.

You don't have time to feel sorry for yourself.

With no day promised, living each one to its fullest is guaranteed to chip away at the beast of *Insecurity* until one day it is a slain dragon which lives only in your memory.

Here are the affirmations that help me slay my dragon:

ELEVEN PERSONAL KEYS TO
SLAYING THE BEAST OF INSECURITY

1. No one wants to hear a failure story. Build your own success story—from the inside out.

2. There are lessons to be learned in everything. Don't let circumstances rob you of your joy.

3. God made all things different—for all time. Each of us has special and unique gifts. This means you too—gift wrapped!

4. The past does not regulate the future. You can change your course by changing your mind.

5. Don't get so carried away with your dream that you forget your own reality. Remember, every fantasy has its price. You've got to pay to get into Disneyland.

6. Suffering is not permanent and pain is not personal.

7. Jealousy is like a withered branch. It is ugly, useless and only works to defeat the rest of a healthy tree.

8. Become a *tryaholic*; not a *failureholic*.

9. Don't think you are crazy if you have a new idea. Just remember that every new idea seems crazy at first. If it weren't crazy someone would have already thought of it.

10. You can see the parade on television. But you can't smell the flowers without being there. Get involved.

11. Angels come! Believe, and create a soft place in your life for them to land.

CHAPTER **3**

THE 4-1-1 ON ATTRACTING ATTENTION:

A HOW TO & WHERE TO PRIMER

❧ Flirting is in, in the '90s.

Have you noticed how some women flirt? Not just with their eyes or their smile. The best flirtation is like swinging a tennis racquet, throwing a bowling ball or executing a golf stroke. A woman who has mastered the art of flirting throws her whole body into it.

A wink. A nod. A casual look—eyes big and bright, focused.

Head gently tossed. Hair fresh and clean.

She swings—like trees in the tropics—to the rhythm of her own nature. She is cool. She is refreshing.

Nothing tense. No frozen parts.

She's not in a do-or-die contest, mind you, to get male attention. She's not competing. With anyone. The girl is just having fun and going with the flow.

You get the feeling that she's enjoying herself more than she is enjoying the attention she is attracting.

Done right—with ease—flirting is an art form. And it is oh, so much fun.

Men love women who can flirt. They can't get enough of it.

It's like a tasty appetizer, a little mouth moistener before the feast.

Sometimes I observe a group of women at a party or business function. All appear to be equally attractive, well dressed, personable, intelligent. But one has the attention of all the men.

She is obviously holding court. And loving it.

She doesn't care if you love her or loathe her. It is Life that she embraces.

Instead of riding this Sister, Girlfriend, let's learn something from her.

🐛   🐛   🐛

One day my salon was lit up on the subject of women with extreme sex appeal. Tastes ranged from Jane Fonda to Sheryl Lee Ralph. From Florence Griffith-Joyner to Whitney Houston. From Angela Lansbury to Whoopi Goldberg.

Suddenly a confident young actress brought the gentlemen in their high-back shine chairs to silence when she announced, "Any woman can be as sexy as any star. All she needs is balls.

"Admit it," she cajoled, "the woman with balls is the one you want to put in your pocket."

The gentlemen were aghast. She laughed.

"Believe you're the finest thing walking," she said, "and you are the finest thing walking. What is that but balls?"

The Sister wasn't really making a question.

She was making a point.

That's not profound, I said to myself. But what was profound I had to admit, was the attention the Sister was attracting. The Brothers sat in rapt attention, hanging on her every word. And every pause.

I think the Sister walked away with two or three phone numbers that day.

🐛   🐛   🐛

I am convinced that men smell confidence, like a vampire smells blood or a dog smells meat. No matter what he says, man is carnivorous. It's in the species.

Let's pause on that *confidence* thing for a minute. Self-confidence that is.

Self-confidence is not needing constant reassurance on your being okay. You neither need nor require the approval of another, no matter how significant that other is.

A friend of mine, as a young woman, was a natural athlete.

A track star. Yes, star! She was one of the most gifted sprinters in her state, a hands-down contender for the Olympics.

She devoted her life to track and field—developing healthy habits and the discipline to perform with excellence.

Most of us girls called her a tomboy but the boys certainly got a kick out of her energy and spunk. Her muscular body was a *firecracker*, the guys joked.

She had at least five big brothers—the most gorgeous hunks on the track team, to the envy of the rest of us girls on the bench.

Until she stumbled into the vice of Love, my friend was a sure bet. A winner. She was admired for her self-confidence and independence.

Her new boyfriend, however, insisted that his lady act more like a lady.

"Wear flattering shoes sometimes. Your legs look deformed in those old grandma shoes," he said.

That was only his first suggestion.

"... And do something with your hair!"

"Listen," he said, after several months of heavy dating, "that track thing is taking up too much of your time."

[I wondered if he could have been jealous of my girl's five big brothers?]

"Why don't you give sports a rest and give us some time? You're so good that one semester won't matter..."

Well, the shot and the put of this story is that my friend did give up track to please her man.

Faster than you can say "final lap" she got pregnant. With the baby came the realization that her track career was over and, in her eyes, the Brother was to blame.

Quite soon after, the relationship was dissolved.

Girlfriend today is the hard-working single mother of two kids—tired and struggling; all of the freshness beat out of her like a high school practice track.

Her trophy room tarnished by bitterness, my friend, while still attractive, is no longer interesting to male suitors. She no longer exudes the graceful self-confidence of a winner.

❦ ❦ ❦

Everybody loves a winner.

Winners are interesting. We all enjoy their stories of limb-climbing and triumph over adversity.

When you lose your winning edge, you often lose your competitive edge besides.

While we're on the subject of winners, let me tell you about a gal who is now a successful dress designer.

This terrific single mom never felt sorry for herself, even when she was left by her husband of 15 years, with four small children.

She had only a high school education and no job.

What she *did* have was self-confidence.

[She wasn't afraid to bust a move.]

So, she moved into a modest apartment, took a menial job and cut back wherever she could in order to make ends meet.

She began her designing career as a means to clothe her kids inexpensively. With scraps of material she would make something wild and imaginative. Then, with the scraps of scraps she'd create something original for herself.

Together, this poor little family looked like a box of broken crayons.

Some people, I'm sure, laughed. But Girlfriend got so good at her patchwork designs she was asked to make some originals for a few neighbors and church friends. She was developing a following.

From a small group of patrons, she was able to buy better fabrics and modern equipment, attracting more and higher paying customers.

Customers, admirers and eventually suitors. From suitors to a steady love. From a steady love to marriage.

I asked her husband of three years what had first attracted her to him and he said, without pausing, "Her self-confidence makes her more alive than any woman I've ever met. That's what makes her so interesting."

To attract positive male attention a woman must be alive. And she must be interesting.

Interesting doesn't mean you have to memorize the latest Dow Jones averages or have a Ph.D. in Geophysics. Interesting just means being involved in Life. Not dwelling on your personal tragedies. Taking the lumps with the sugar with aplomb.

Speaking of lumps, my Sister, we are not camels with our lumps out there for inspection. We've all got some bruises.

When you are hurting, you don't need the world to hurt with you. A Brother who likes to dance through life will certainly not want to accept an invitation to your pity party.

Learn to have a sense of humor about yourself, whatever your circumstances. You and your circumstances can change.

Now that you've got the *how* of attracting positive male attention, let's talk about the *where.*

Where you go to meet a decent Brother these days is almost as important as being open to accept a positive relationship in the first place.

Obviously you won't attract the same kind of attention in a bar as you will in a bowling alley.

Bowling alley?

Listen, Girlfriend, a bowling alley is a great place to meet a big league player. Bowling alleys are the great melting pot of the male workforce. Practically every tenured bus driver, postal worker and longshoreman I know belongs to a bowling league.

Speaking of bowling alleys, the least likely place to meet a decent catch is often the best place.

Not that you can't meet a great guy in a bar, but the chances are pretty slim. Men come there, like you did, for the catch-action. On the bar scene you'll usually find women vying for male attention like groupies at a rock concert.

You can do better in places rarely frequented by women trying to get over. Like the bowling alley. Or the pool hall.

Or how about the barber shop?

You don't need a hair cut and you don't have a son, you say?

Well, rent-a-son for a Saturday morning. Take your nephew or friend's son for a hair cut and afterwards, breakfast at McDonald's.

You'll be doing a tired mom a service and maybe

snip a little bonus for yourself.

Barber shops and shoe shine parlors—on Thursday, Friday or Saturday—are great places to meet progressive men who are about something.

Now, I mentioned shoe shines before, but now let me give you the 4-1-1 on this mecca of maledom.

Brothers who keep their shoes shined either have a job or they're looking pretty darned hard for one. They are ambitious. They have an agenda. They are about something.

Find the most popular shoe shine parlor in your town and you'll also find the epicenter of the Brotherhood. Make yourself a regular. Don't be afraid to hop up into the arms of that comfortable high-backed leather chair for a shine.

For a couple of bucks you'll feel relaxed and look great from head to toe. And just think of the positive attention you'll be attracting.

Sure, some women may stare at you disapprovingly. But that's just because they don't have the nerve to take center stage.

To tell you the truth, Brothers are fascinated by Sisters who don't care what other women think. They know that the approval of our Sisterhood is the staple diet of our gender.

[Just think, all our gossip about a Sister is not doing anything but making her more intriguing to our men.]

❦   ❦   ❦

While we're talking about gossip, my Sister, if you want to attract attention of the best kind, stay clear of poison words about anybody—your ex, your relatives, the woman across the street.

Any man worth his weight in cashmere knows that the cowardly lion roars the loudest.

He'll figure, and rightfully so, that a woman who talks about other people, while trying to butter him up, will spread the word on him too.

The best way to attract positive attention is to be joyous to the world, starting with yourself.

A happy tree bares healthy fruit.

And bad grapes produce bitter wine.

Now, back to that shoe shine parlor...or barber shop... or bowling alley. In the process of meeting new people you are also establishing new relationships and expanding your network of acquaintances.

As you build new relationships, one or two of them may turn into genuine friendships. So if you've not met a love interest at least you've met someone of interest. And who knows who he knows. Maybe the Brother has a friend. Or a cousin. Maybe the Brother has a brother!

❧   ❧   ❧

Want some more unlikely places to meet men? Everyone's hip to church. That's what I call the Old Standard. But have you ever thought of funerals?

I'm not trying to sound morbid. I'm really not! It

just seems to me that death, everybody's final chapter, is definitely a part of life.

You can't avoid it. So why avoid the thoughtful tradition of paying your respects to the departed and to the bereaved?

Along with grieving family members, funeral services are also comprised of the friends, business associates and co-workers of the deceased who have come to bid farewell. That means they are still very much alive.

[Why, those pews are virtually crawling with live ones!]

Along with bowling alleys, barber shops, shine parlors, funeral services and wakes, I'd have to rank computer, camera and electronic retail stores, car washes, garage sales, laundromats, supermarkets, and libraries (science and business sections) as my favorite places to meet interesting men.

It has also been suggested, by my sporty girlfriends, that high school, YMCA and pro basketball games; golf, riding and rifle ranges offer great action on and off the court.

All of these spots offer one thing: they are places you can chat and get to know each other a tad, without a swarm of women trying to make your private conversation a party line.

Party line. That reminds me of a theory proffered by a friend of mine, a vivacious lady who returned to school, at age 41, for her law degree. She calls it the Catch A Fish theory.

She says, quite simply, "You can't catch a fish in a

bathtub. You have to get out there, in the deep water, where you can't touch bottom. The scarcest fish is in the deepest water but it also brings the biggest prize."

Please believe me, on any given four-hour fishing expedition in a bar with your girlfriends only one of you is likely to catch a live one.

So challenge me!

Reduce your odds of coming up with an old spare tire by fishing alone or at least in discreet company.

🐛   🐛   🐛

Your goal, my Sister, is to attract positive attention. Start by being positive. Don't just go anywhere. Go somewhere. And go with gusto and great relish.

Enthusiasm for who you are—what you're about and what you're into—are the things that make you an attractive attention-getter.

If you really want to attract male attention you can drive a Beemer or a VW minibus. You can shop at designer salons or thrift shops. You don't need to do or say anything extraordinary to impress him. Just loosen up and relax and enjoy a Brother's attention, regardless of where you think it may lead.

Be feminine, attentive and alive. You will attract more quality male attention than you ever imagined possible.

CHAPTER 4

PICKING & CHOOSING or ONE WOMAN'S HASH IS ANOTHER'S GOURMET FEAST

 You can't make a pot of chili without having the ingredients.

And you won't have all the ingredients until you go to the store.

Ladies, the market shelves are well stocked. Please don't settle for the first hunk of hamburger you set your sights on.

Now, this is a tough one for some Sisters—even in the midst of today's AIDS Terror.

My mother used to tell me, and most mother's still tell their sexually curious daughters, "Keep your panties on."

"But I love him," you say.

As Tina Turner asked so eloquently, *"What does love have to do with it?"*

A Catholic nun, of all things, once shared with me the secret of a successful marriage: "Select a partner with the qualities you most desire in a mate," she said. "Throw out the "L" word entirely. If he makes you happy—satisfying your personal needs—believe me, you'll fall in love with him."

I followed this divine logic in considering my second husband; accepting his proposal even though I didn't love him in that boom-boom way that makes your blood rush.

He was a nice man and a great friend who made me laugh. We had wonderful, adventurous fun and we had much in common. I didn't love him but I really *liked* him.

Within a month of being married—as we planned our belated honeymoon to Rio de Janeiro for Carnival—I fell in love with this kind and thoughtful man. That love only grew in time and never wavered.

We had a successful marriage for ten years, until other obstacles loomed.

❦   ❦   ❦

Now that you have his attention, it's time to examine why you're seeking it in the first place.

Is he really the one you want or are you just window shopping at the After Christmas sale?

Now you know, Girlfriend, that we have a bad habit of buying a pair of shoes just because they're cute and in style, our girlfriend likes them or they are on sale.

If they hurt, we may only wear them once. Or we'll wait to buy a perfect dress to match. Usually, though, those expensive brand new shoes will sit in the back of the closet until we give them away.

Let's be honest. Sometimes a Sister will treat a man like those cute pair of new shoes that she really didn't want in the first place. If you do anything more than try him on, yours is strictly a vanity move.

You may like him [someday]. But you know you're wrong to be using the poor fellow to catch Mr. Right.

[Am I wrong?]

What goes around comes around.

So now you finally meet someone interesting. You like the Brother and you think he has the same feelings for you.

You think you are his girlfriend but you may only be an amusing diversion from his problems at work, problems at home or problems with people.

To this rakish rogue you are just a pair of "cute shoes."

❧ ❧ ❧

One attractive and wealthy gentleman, whom I adored, used to take me to expensive restaurants four or five times a week.

I thought he genuinely loved me.

The truth was that he genuinely loved to eat, and I was good company—like a fine linen napkin.

Some men hate to eat alone!

Some men hate to do anything alone. You are only in their lives to fill up the empty spaces.

One of my greatest loves was such a man. After six months of blissful dating he began to pick arguments out of me, like a cat owner picking fur balls out of the sofa.

Suddenly I could do nothing right. Nothing pleased him. He was truly unhappy.

I discovered that he really loved the shifting sands of chaos. For a short time I was, for him, the large smooth rocks in the stream that he used to keep his feet dry.

He finally married a lady who satisfied his insatiable hunger for pain. She was a sweet young Georgia peach-of-a-girl whom he subsequently hospitalized after one of their frequent, nasty spats.

She, in turn, upon her release and return home, tried to fry him in hot chicken grease while he slept.

Wake up, Ladies, and smell the roses. The garden holds more than a hundred varieties. You don't have to settle for artificial flowers. You don't have to be miserable in a relationship.

"A man, at any cost," my Sister, is a strategy out of the 1950's that our mothers used to earn that house with a white picket fence.

This is the '90s and most of us live in apartments, condos and townhouses anyway. Isn't it time to choose to be in a satisfying relationship?

❦　　❦　　❦

Some ladies only pick men who are inaccessible. Married men, gay men, priests, just-divorced men are all clearly inaccessible.

Yet some Sisters seem Hell-bent on chasing these Brothers.

Like a piece of ripening fruit, you can usually tell a man who is pickable. He is: generally honest about his involvements, usually open to suggestions on how you spend your time together, and always enjoys your company. He returns your affections in equal or greater measure.

I have a friend who has been in love with more married men than there are pigeons on a playground. She says that's not her intention. But when we sat down to talk about the dilemma that seemed to keep her mascara running, she broke down.

It was the mystique of chasing a man who didn't want her that was the turn-on and the challenge.

Her "high" came from being near a man who was just out of reach.

Many women thrive on the chase. They don't want a man who has his feet planted on the ground. These Sisters seem to deliberately choose:

— The *Benz-o drivin' Lady Killer,*
  whose black book looks like the Manhattan Yellow Pages.
— The *Professional Man* whose every sentence starts with "I."
— The *Career Criminal*
  or *Chronically Unemployed.*
— The long suffering, *Tormented Alcoholic or Drug Addict.*
— The *Pathetic Puppy* whose luck just won't change.

— The neat-to-the-bone *Eternal Bachelor.*
— The *Married-to-Mama Man,* or his cousin,
   the *My-Kids-Can-Do-No-Wrong Parent-Man.*

Don't think I'm talking Psych. 101 here, good Sisters. I've been in relationships with all of these untouchables. And I have the battle scars to prove it.

❧   ❧   ❧

My nemesis seems to be the *Pathetic Puppy* type. They aren't overtly mean or insensitive. They are chameleon-type men who appear to be normal nice guys. They are nice guys who, unfortunately, have been kicked so hard by life they have permanent hoof marks on their egos.

One recent beau, whom I simply adored, had been an abused husband for 17 years. Although divorced for the last six years, he recounted past historical atrocities as if they'd been in yesterday's newspaper.

Every now and then he'd go on a tirade. The memory of his unfaithful wife would suddenly cloud our pleasant present moments.

The more he relaxed with me, the more he'd experience psychedelic flashbacks to his tormented past relationship.

One night, in a casual dinner setting, as I was suggesting items on the menu, he shouted, "Shut up!"

I knew it wasn't me he was talking to; but rather the ghost of his nagging and deceitful ex-wife. But still, who can compete with a ghost? I'm not in the exorcism business.

Another fine, robust and intelligent friend of mine was caught up in job stress. Once again he appeared to be normal. But on further inspection, there were tire marks across the face of his self-esteem that looked like a bumper car ride at Tinkertown.

[Screech!]

The closer we got, the more comfortable he was with taking me on his bumpy ride of rejection by Corporate America. Slipping in and out of his horror story, he put on the brakes only to tell me how he planned to get even.

I had to turn him off just to keep my own engine running.

If you pick a *Pathetic Puppy*, be sure, my Sister, you are ready to provide constant maternal vigilance.

These guys are never housebroken and will not hesitate to tinkle on your rug. They are never sorry but they are always pitiful.

And when you abandon them, expect to be charged with inhumane treatment and animal endangerment.

🐾   🐾   🐾

Now before we leave the kennel, Girlfriend, and the downside of our choices, let's talk about the *Dog Catcher*. That's what I call ladies whose only experiences are with heels, jerks and ne're-do-wells who will take a Sister for anything (and everything) they can get.

I hear the horror stories from all sides: The dogs who only pimp broads, the ladies who are being treated like bitches; and the nice guys who try to rescue them.

If he is a big spender, flashy dresser or a charismatic fast-talker, those are just a few signs that your new show dog may still belong in the kennel.

Now here's my famous *Dog Catcher Quiz* designed to spot a Sister who always attracts men who are heartbreakers:

ARE YOU A DOG CATCHER???

1. Are you into thrills (which does not necessarily mean adventure)?

2. Are you bored if he doesn't have a good line?

3. Does your first date or first kiss have to crinkle your toes and turn your brain to mush?

4. Would you rather have his money than his time?

5. Does his car, house, dog or job impress you?

---

6. Are you into Power (with a capital "P")?

7. Does his style hold more of your attention than his smile?

8. Does it bother you if he stutters, stammers or is clumsy when he tells you how much he cares for you?

9. Does being laid mean more to you than being loved?

10. Would you rather have his gold than share his goals?

If you answer "yes" to any one of the above questions I'd seriously look at myself as a possible *Dog Catcher.* You're inviting trouble in your own backyard.

My advice is to have a Brother tested for rabies before you take him home to play with the kids.

🐾 🐾 🐾

I have found some truth to the homespun adage "You get what you deserve." You definitely attract what you want by affirming it in thought, word, and action.

And listen, Girlfriend, don't put a label or a name on your eventual soulmate. Be open and flexible. You think he's *the one* today, but Mr. Tom, Richard or Hakim may not be your intended life's partner in the thousand tomorrows ahead of you.

Our picture is limited to what we see at the present moment. God's picture is the Universe for all the time that was, is and ever will be. Now who do you trust?

There is someone for everyone. In fact, there is more than one someone for everyone. To prove it, look at your own life's experiences. How many times have you loved someone so hard you thought you would break if they didn't love you back?

And when you didn't break and didn't die, but lived to love again, weren't you a tad surprised?

[Come on, Girl, admit it.]

In my little corner of the world I personally know hundreds of fine eligible men of all ages, races and pro-fessions—many looking for meaningful relationships.

If mine is any kind of sample, I am sure that there is someone for everyone!

It is your life. It is your choice. Today, pick this moment to be happy. Choose this time to be accessible to the good that is waiting for you around the corner.

And while you negotiate the twists and turns along the highway of life, I wish you happy motoring, my Sister. May you enjoy safe driving conditions to your destination.

CHAPTER 5

"NICE"

∿ There is a lot of ambivalence about nice guys. There is, in fact, ambivalence about *nice* anything.

Far from being a virtue, *nice* is often used in today's vernacular in place of "odd."

"That's a nice dress you're wearing," doesn't mean that your dress is pretty, sexy or fashionable. "Nice" usually means that it looks like your dress is a third-generation hand-me-down. Or you bought it at a Salvation Army fire sale.

A nice car is cheap. A nice house is one no one else would want to live in.

When a friend suggests you meet her nice friend you already know that he is boring and predictable. .

A nice guy is the guy you love to hate. He is the nerd who hangs on you and around you until you kick him out of your life.

Nice guys finish last. If they finish at all.

When you are in a stormy relationship with another man it is the nice guy who is always your *incidental target*. You were aiming at someone else but the nice guy accidentally got in your line of fire. So he took the bullet.

You didn't mean to hurt his feelings... to stand him up... to forget his birthday... It's just that something better came up.

If you've got some ambivalent feelings about *nice* guys, you are in good company.

The ambivalence you feel probably stems from the confusion promulgated by the lexicographers themselves. Lexicographers, you see, spend their entire careers researching words, their meaning and derivatives.

The great Noah Webster defines *nice* as "difficult to please; fastidious; refined."

It is only way down the line, definition number six, does he say that nice is "agreeable; pleasant; and delightful."

That's what Webster says.

The word comes from the Latin "Nescius" which means ignorant; not knowing.

Other dictionaries, like the *Oxford American* defines nice as "pleasant, satisfactory."

My thesaurus says that nice is "agreeable; amicable; congenial and friendly."

Is that confusing, or what?

I mean, if the people writing the dictionaries these days can't make up their minds on the meaning of "nice," how the heck can we?

Maybe our root confusion over nice guys stems from our confusion over the root of the word "nice."

You say he's so nice; but maybe you mean that he's so ignorant. Remember *Nescius?*

That nice guy presents quite a dilemma for my Sisters.

Every normal, breathing single Sister says she is looking for a nice guy. Yet, when she finds him, she treats him like the best friend of a new bride who tags along on the honeymoon.

Sure he's a man with feelings and she doesn't really want to lose him. But then, on the other hand, she wonders why he hangs around where he's not wanted.

Another problem with nice guys: because they're there, it's tempting to do unto them as you've been done into.

If you're being jerked around by some heel, sometimes you just have to give someone else the boot!

A nice guy tells you that he is willing to wait forever for you to return his affections. You want to scream, "That's exactly how long it will take."

The jerks, women and the nice guys themselves all agree on one thing. Nice guys get no respect.

"Nice" today means a Brother is gullible; stupid and conspicuously accessible.

No wonder they finish last.

🦂 🦂 🦂

Maybe it's time to get this "nice" thing straight.

A nice guy is one who takes you dancing. A nice guy will go with you to walk the dog. He doesn't mind seeing your hair in rollers. He brings his money home. He listens.

One contented Sister told me that her nice guy is considerate of her time, feelings and goals.

Another, a high-strung musician, claims that what makes her nice guy so special is his tolerance of her many moods.

Not one of these Sisters would look at another man. They love being treated grandly.

I have several friends who married nice guys. To tell the truth—to a woman—they've never been happier.

How they met their Mr. Nice Guy varied but all of these Sisters agreed that they picked up some other woman's leavings.

[Leftovers.]

He was banged around by another Sister so badly that he hid from women by spending all his free time working on his car or buffing up at the gym.

Nice guys, in the '90s, are so discouraged they have all but taken themselves out of the race to attract nice ladies. They've grown so quiet we hardly know they still exist.

Darned that old Webster! He's got our relationships all screwed up.

Nice guys make the best catches. There is no contest. Not only is a nice guy a pleasant enough fellow to be around, he is available.

And there is a big bonus. A nice Brother stopped looking for perfection long ago. You don't have to constantly dazzle him or use all your energy to confound him. He just wants a lady who will treat him with a little respect.

There are a lot of nice guys out there, my Sister, if only you'll change your *himpressions* about what *nice* means to you.

If you have a nice Brother scoping you out, you had better put on your glasses. Please learn to pamper him before some other sharp-eyed Sister with 20/20 vision sets her sights on him.

CHAPTER 6

IF YOU WERE A...
THE MAN BEHIND THE MASK

ॐ You are introduced to a man who seems too good to be true. You hit it off immediately. You have so much in common. He's perfect!

But then we all have stories about a dream date turned into a nightmare. How could you have been so wrong about him? Were there signs you just ignored? Or was he a master of disguise?

Before you get into giving up your time, space and maybe even the key to your front door, you've got to ask yourself, "Is he for real or just another plastic apple in the barrel?" Don't you deserve to know what you're in for before you take a bite?

Now here's a fun little game you can play that may reveal the man behind the mask.

With the *If You Were A...* Game, you don't have to wait to get your heart broken. A careful survey of a Brother's answers, although in fun, may reveal more of the man than the *Emperor's New Clothes*.

The fun part of the *If You Were A...* Game is that it can be played anytime, anywhere—even through half-time during "Monday Night Football."

It's non-threatening and, unless he's read this book, he'll never suspect what you're really up to. Even if he has, there are no right or wrong answers. It's just a matter of preference. The point is, they're your preferences! You are in control.

The *If You Were A...* Game is a cross between "Twenty Questions" and the fill-in-the-blanks quiz you used to take in school. Now, this sample is my own subjective quiz, but feel free to use your own nouns to reveal some surprises that may await you further into your relationship.

IF YOU WERE A...

---

1. If you were a dog, what kind of dog would you be? [Watch out for pit bulls and Doberman pincers. Remember too, the more exotic the breed the more expensive the vet bill.]

2. If you were a flower, what kind of flower would you be? [Some flowers wilt before you get them home. They're only pretty in the box.]

3. If you were a bird, what kind of bird would you be? [Do I need to warn you about vultures or buzzards?!]

4. If you were an insect, which one would you be? [Some insects nurture plants, like bees and ladybugs. Others, like mosquitoes and roaches, carry disease.]

5. If you were a spice, which spice would you be? [Your warning flag should be at full mast if he says "pepper."]

6. If you were a car, what kind of car would you be? [Show-off cars, like Benzos and Porsches, get stolen; Caddys and Lincs hog the road. You may be better off looking for something that's sleek, safe and economical.]

7. If you were a color, what color would you be? [Seeing red—feeling blue—turning green—acting yellow? Any of these can turn your mood to black even if you're generally in the pink.]

8. If you were a piece of fruit, which one would you be? [If peach fuzz makes you itch, try a nectarine. One day in the sun will do a banana in. Sturdy fruit like apples and oranges are great to take on picnics. They don't squish or change colors.]

(continued on next page)

9. If you were a fabric, which fabric would you be? [Most ladies in the '90s are into natural fibers like cotton and wool blends. Rayon and polyester are as popular as a '60s leisure suit.]

10. If you were a flavor of ice cream, what flavor would you be? [No man in his right mind will answer this one with "Tuitty Fruity." But better take a hard look at Rocky Road, Almond Fudge and Pistachio too. There are some real nuts out there.]

11. If you were a piece of architecture, what would you be? [Dungeons and castles are a good sign that he's into domination. Gothic is cold and ranch tells you he's a sprawler. Could your couch potato's stack of empty beer cans be far behind?]

12. If you were a cartoon character, who would you be?, [Most of us have already dated a "Goofy," "Road Runner," "Dumbo," and "Mickey Mouse." I'll take "Roger Rabbit" over "Casper, the Friendly Ghost," anytime.]

13. If you were a type of cheese which one would you be? [Swiss has holes; Muenster is smelly; and Roquefort falls apart. Your Cheddars— mild, medium and sharp; according to taste— are a good bet for being strong, flavorful and on the practical side.]

14. If you were a character in the Bible, who would you be? [Samson was a pushover to Delilah. Some men are martyred John the Baptists. Others have a king complex and you're a subject, or worse, a slave. The next time you meet a king remember—the higher the pedestal the greater the fall.]

15. If you were a letter in the alphabet, which one would you be? ["A" may mean that he's into himself. "Z" usually means that he'll take the last word in any dispute. I like "M," as in middle of the road or masculine.]

16. If you were a wallet what would you be made of? [The tougher the cowhide, the better the leather, I always say.]

(continued on next page)

17. If you were a musical instrument, which one would you be? [Some instruments, I don't need to tell you, are just a lot of wind. Others can bombast you with their roar. Nervous little instruments—like the flute—are hard to tune. Me? Give me a grand piano. I'm into harmony!]

18. If you were a beverage what beverage would you be? [Carbonated or noncarbonated; with or with out caffeine, alcoholic or natural, those are the questions.]

19. If you were a tree, what tree would you be? [Oak trees shed their leaves in the fall. Palm trees don't have leaves and they are nests for rats. Some trees make lousy building materials. Eucalyptus is my choice for a tree that gives shade, has utility and leaves that can be used for medicinal purposes.]

20. If you were a fish which fish would you be? [If he says he'd be a dolphin or a whale you know that he doesn't know what a fish is.]

CHAPTER 7

BEWARE THE FAAWABA!

〜 It helps, when talking about pampering, to understand the antithesis of this fine noble art. To this end I say—BEWARE OF THE FAAWABA.

WARNING: A *Faawaba* is a woman who threatens to undermine the little opportunity other Sisters have to pamper a Brother by totally destroying his trust in all women.

I digress.

To conquer the enemy, you must know who she is.

If you think the *Faawaba* is a species of fierce beast with few predators and an insatiable appetite for living flesh, you'd be perfectly right.

F.A.A.W.A.B.A. That's Ferocious African-American Woman with A Bad Attitude. These Sisters are by no means extinct and in every way dangerous.

I'll start here by pointing the finger back at myself. During periods of great upheaval and personal dissatisfaction I've been a *Faawaba* princess through many relationships.

Since I speak from some experience, I can tell you that a *Faawaba* is not someone you want to mess with.

She will give you headaches and strokes; make you lose your hair or your mind. She is a Jezebel, without any mask of propriety.

For the purposes of distinguishing *Faawabas* from the rest of our gentle gender I've invented a little check list which, if followed, will warn you against getting caught in her snare or of becoming, yourself, the dreaded *Faawaba*.

You see, one of the important goals of this *Guide* is to identify the pamperable (of both sexes) as opposed to those Brothers and Sisters who will hurt you or take extreme advantage of you with a quickness.

Breaking an old code of silence I am compelled, both as a writer and a recovering *Faawaba*, to share some of her secrets.

---

23 CHARACTERISTICS
OF A GENUINE FAAWABA

1. She doesn't listen. She's too busy complaining.

2. She can't be satisfied.

3. She never apologizes for being late and always blames you for being early.

---

4. She audits your time and charges you for hers.

5. She is happiest when you're miserable.

6. She gloats.

7. She rarely shows gratitude or appreciation for anything without a price tag.

8. She constantly compares you to her last husband, lover or father.

9. She blames anyone [and everyone] for her problems and shortcomings.

10. She changes voices—depending on to whom she is speaking.

11. She is loud at inappropriate times.

12. She can't stand hearing another Sister's good news.

13. She holds grudges against others into the next millennium.

(continued on next page)

14. She answers your questions with a question.

15. She hates eating alone. She hates being alone.

16. She insults you in public. She hangs up on you in private.

17. She is passionate only about negative things.

18. She can't accept criticism and she can't give praise.

19. She cries to excuse her bad behavior.

20. She makes fun of you or laughs at you.

21. While making love, she just lays there.

22. She fusses, cusses, never discusses.

23. She sulks.

A genuine *Faawaba* is totally engrossed in her own performance. She wouldn't stomp on a grape wearing a pair of Army boots; but she'll come to your party and drink all the wine.

I've also noticed that a *Faawaba* is into self-mutilation.

She wears 20-pounds of nylon braids woven tightly into her scalp; three-inch acrylic fingernails with rhinestoned pinky fingers; two pairs of humongous gold-plated pierced earrings and a diamond nose stud; and crippling four-inch red vinyl Stiletto heels.

[Maybe its the pain that makes her so mean.]

🐞　🐞　🐞

Now I'll admit that most Sisters have a little *Faawaba* mixed in their blood. [Every woman does, regardless of her race.]

It's the fallout from *Faawabas* that bothers me. *Faawabas* give *all* Sisters a bad name.

A White woman who has a bad day or acts outrageous is perceived as out-of-sorts or going through PMS.

Even though *Faawabas* come in all colors, nobody thinks of a White woman as a "*Ferocious Anglo-American Woman with A Bad Attitude.*"

Black Sisters get no such break.

When an otherwise mild-mannered Blackwoman gets her feathers ruffled she is merely living *down* to expectations.

The Faawabas amongst us have made it nearly impossible for any Sister to have legitimate rage least her Blackman say, "Now there you go. You're acting just like a *Blackwoman.*"

He doesn't mean you, Girlfriend. That's the *Faawaba* he's talking about.

That is why I say let us unmask the dreaded *Faawabas* and let the real Sisters shine.

❦ ❦ ❦

Okay, so I'm a little down on *Faawabas*. But let me explain why.

See, *Faawabas* have frequently gotten the best of me in matters of men, jobs and the loyalties of other friends. They always seem to stand [or lie] in the way.

One day I wondered why *Faawabas* seem to have every advantage. And privilege.

I mean, if there were a contest between a *Faawaba* and a gentle Sister, the *Faawaba* would show up late and still win.

Suddenly I realized that *Faawabas* make great bitches because they practice.

Gentle Sisters are just gentle. They don't work at being real or kind or anything. They just are.

Faawabas work at their witchcraft until they have it perfected to a fine art. [No wonder many a great gal comes in second place.]

To tell the truth, I've never known a *Faawaba* who wasn't good at: picking a fight (on her turf or yours, but always on her own terms); embarrassing an intended victim; or just leaving. [She'll walk in a minute.]

We may not understand the allure of this Sepia femme fatale, but we've got to respect her. She's a tough act to beat and even tougher to follow.

You see, a *Faawaba* captivates her man before she castrates him. Then she decapitates him.

After she's full and satisfied, his memory is nothing more than a belch. [Have mercy!]

When a *Faawaba* turns her man out, she'll throw his clothes in the street or burn them. She'll charge him with rape. She'll call his friends, his family *and* his boss with her character assassinations.

If she's a friend of yours, count on her loyalty only at her convenience. [*Faawabas* generally make lousy friends.]

❦ ❦ ❦

On the positive side of the balance sheet it's good to know that if you are being victimized by a *Faawaba*—in friendship or in love—you can do something about it. You can: a) Leave [as in pack up and split]; or b) Help her to see herself as she really is.

If you choose the latter and you want to preserve your sanity, you must perform a *Faawabasism* as quickly as possible. [I'm telling you, you've got to exorcise those demons!]

A *Faawaba-sism* is unplastic surgery—that is personality reconstruction by removing all the plastic. Now here's one quick *Faawabasism* that should scare the unholy *Faawaba* out of the Sister in a few weeks.

THE FIVE-STEP FAAWABASISM

1. When she starts acting ugly, toss a mirror up in front of her face. This forces the Faawaba to see herself as she really is.

2. Secretly tape record the Faawaba's next tirade and spring it on her when she comes to you normal.

3. When she tries to bite your head off, throw her a dog biscuit.

4. Warn her that you're going to blow a whistle on her bad behavior. Every time she acts up, do just that. Blow it loud.

5. Reward her for each day of good behavior with a little treat. If she makes it through an entire week without an outburst, make it a big treat.

If you are a practicing *Faawaba* and have run off every man close to you, you may wish to perform a *Self-Faawabasism*. Just like self-hypnosis. You've got to relax and get inside yourself. Become aware of what you are thinking, how you are acting and how others are perceiving you.

All the power you gave to creating evil you can give to creating joy. [I promise you, it is a better high to make people smile than to make them cry.]

If your goal is to have a Blackman beating down your door, begging to be pampered, teach the *Faawaba* side of your personality some control. Take her to finishing school. Form a 12-Step recovery group with other admitted *Faawabas*. Check your *Faawaba* coat of arms at the door.

Every Sister has the capacity to turn the *Faawaba* in her to a W.A.A.W.A.B.A. That's <u>W</u>onderful <u>A</u>frican <u>A</u>merican <u>W</u>oman with <u>A</u> <u>B</u>right <u>A</u>ttitude. If only she will learn to give a little, bend a little and share a lot.

CONDOMPHOBIA & INTIMACY
IN THE AIDS GENERATION

⌒ Growing older, that old biological clock ticking down the years, often makes us cling to the next man you meet who smiles and speaks English.

Don't let the Brother have a job and be single!

The Sisters jump the Brother like a hawk jumps on a wounded chicken.

Jumping on him, my Sister, or letting him jump on you is, these days, as dangerous as playing footsies with a rattle snake in your sleeping bag.

This is the AIDS Generation; not the '60s, when it was cool to go from the streets to the sheets in one easy night.

There's just nothing easy about sex these days. The threat of AIDS has taken the fun out of fun 'n' games.

In the '90s you can't afford to trip on sex like a summer vacation. A romp or two and then you're through. Nowadays every season of promiscuity carries a possible death sentence.

Not enough people are talking about sex these days outside of the talk show circuit. Not even in the bedroom. Most folks aren't talking; they are just doing it.

Still doing IT! I don't get it.

I mean, this is the AIDS Generation, Girlfriend, and we've been pounded with enough warning information by the media to all be well-informed. It is obvious to me that in the AIDS Generation, people are not getting the message.

Some Brothers are in strong denial of AIDS or any other incurable disease. To these sexual gladiators, life is still a continual sexual feast, even after the "Magic revelation" of 1991.

Sadly, many of these warriors of wanderlust are Brothers of means. In fact, it is their money that gives them the means to enjoy the fruits of their affluence to the fullest.

Sex, for these gents, is a status symbol—right along with membership in the country club, the Mercedes Benz, Bali shoes and the American Express Gold card.

Some men change women like most people change their socks.

I'm not talking just single satyrs either, my Sister. I'm talking married [with children] men and men in [otherwise] committed relationships.

It seems that most guys today don't believe AIDS can catch them with their pants down.

And they are not alone. Many Sisters are going to get caught with their skirts up too.

Some Sisters, I've noticed, are afraid not to do IT. There are so many Sisters who will do IT and so few Brothers who don't demand IT that some Sisters feel they have to give IT up to get asked to dance.

To these Sisters my question is: If you are *giving* it away, what makes you think he owes you anything?

[Free is free. Right?]

Other Sisters do IT to pay the rent or the car note. Or, to eat in a gourmet restaurant; to get invited to an exclusive party; to ride in a fine car. They're not hooking, really. They've just got a financial agenda. Sex is nothing more than currency.

In a growing number of cases, Sisters are afraid of the reduction of lifestyle after a divorce. They don't want to lose the car, give up the house or take the kid out of private school.

To lose a man is one thing; to lose a credit card is quite another. So they buy time by selling their bodies and selling their lives.

Still walking amongst us are the slutty Sisters who will still give IT up faster than a compulsive shopper in a 99-cents store.

And the weekend players who are celibate for whole five-day stretches at a time. They are addicted to love and are drawn to sex like syrup to a pancake. They soak it up and never get enough.

It is amazing to me how many excuses folks use to trivialize sex, without exercising the slightest bit of caution.

It seems to me that we're more cautious about how we eat than with whom we sleep.

[You wouldn't eat with someone else's fork, would you?]

I'm no prude, but abstinence to me makes good health sense in the '90s. But for those who do IT, do IT right. [Pretty please.]

For his sake and for your sake, carry a condom as close to you as your lipstick. And use it with the same regularity.

Condoms are as essential to lovemaking in the '90s as birth control pills were in the '60s.

Don't leave home without them.

Sadly, buying a condom and using it are two separate issues today. According to some surveys, while most singles talk condoms and safe sex, neither men nor women actually use protection.

Men in heat don't think about condoms as part of their wardrobe. And women, who do carry condoms, are often too embarrassed to use them.

Even in the '90s it's Monkey Business as usual.

With AIDS on the rise in the heterosexual Black community, I am led to conclude that we suffer from a new disease—*Condomphobia*—or, the fear of condoms. Far too many Brothers and Sisters are scared to use condoms.

Some simply play Russian Roulette with their lives. But most people just don't seem to think about the lethal ramifications of their sexual actions.

Do you realize that more men and women lie about their sexual history to prospective partners than they do about their income to the IRS?

[Told any recent fish stories yourself, Girlfriend?]

❧   ❧   ❧

Say he's married. And he's screwing around with you!
Are you the only Sister he's fooling around with? And
do you insist that he use a condom *every* time you
make love?

Okay, now say you're the wife of a man who is
fooling around. [Are you fooling around too, by the
way?]

Oh yes, and do you always insist on condom use
with your spouse? With your lover?

Sadly, far too many Brothers and Sisters suffering
from *Condomphobia* are still in denial of the AIDS epidemic. They are clearly out of touch with the AIDS
Generation. And today being out of touch is a terminal
mistake.

AIDS, as a growing number of heterosexuals can
testify, is a family disease and an equal opportunity
killer.

❧   ❧   ❧

Girlfriend, Girlfriend, if you want to pamper your
Blackman, protect him and yourself from the ultimate
death sentence. Be the first Sister in your circle of
friends to insist on protection.

Your man may protest. He may object. The Brother
may tell you that he hasn't had sex in six years—since

he left the monastery. He *knows* he's safe. He wonders about you. He's hurt that you don't trust him.

He may show you his most recent health certificate and swear on his mother's life that he wouldn't hurt you.

The jury is out on *how* you instantly change your long-held sexual practices. And getting your macho man to accept a "raincoat," even though he thinks the sun is shining, is not without risk. But risk you must.

[Risk the friendship or perish from the plague.]

I've asked hundreds of Sisters how they handle this delicate issue. Most are rather cut and dry. [No pun intended.]

Only one Sister, in fact, so moved me to share her experience.

This Sister admitted that she had been phobic about condoms until a few years ago when she discovered a former lover leaving a gay bar.

"That did it," she declared. "I thought the guy was as straight as a ruler. If I could be wrong about him I could be wrong about anyone."

This conscious woman conquered her phobia overnight. Today she wouldn't be caught dead in bed without a condom.

I asked her how she approached the subject with lovers and other would-be intimate partners.

"When the conversations rolls around to sex," she says, "I tell my companion that story. And I always tell him that it only happened three months ago."

"I look at him sweetly and say, 'Baby, I don't want you to be at risk.'"

Some Brothers, she says, don't mind taking the risk.

"If they'd take a risk on me," she says, "they're definitely too risky for me."

Some Brothers, she says, run an Olympic mile to get away from her. Those men, she figures, aren't worth playing with anyway.

Like the Marines, she figures, she only needs a few good men.

Those are the ones who appreciate her "admission" and will certainly take precautions. These Brothers, she says, even thank her for her honesty and a few come clean themselves.

From a possible tragedy this Sister has constructed a litmus test for intimacy.

Now, I'm sure that there are more subtle [and less devious] ways of enticing your gentleman to use protection.

You might tell him that you've just taken a megadose of fertility pills and unless he wants to be the daddy of sextuplets you advise him to use a condom.

You might bone up on the latest AIDS research and have a few policy papers conveniently placed on the nightstand.

[See *50 Ways to Say No to Sex.*]

Or you might even tell him the truth—that you have no plans to become an AIDS statistic.

The point is that, now, as a member of the AIDS Generation, you can't afford to get cold feet or be weak in the knees on this issue. You've got to take a real stand to conquer *Condomphobia.*

I've found that the easiest way of overcoming any phobia is to reach out and grab ahold of the situation.

If your Brother won't voluntarily change his sexual dressing habits, my hands-on advice to cure him of *Condomphobia* is to get a grip on that bad boy, and take matters into your own hands. The control, dear Sister, is at your fingertips.

Because Himpressions: The Blackwoman's Guide to Pampering The Blackman is truly a users manual, I am duty-bound to share with my Sisters 50 ways of overcoming even the most ardent proposal of *sack-jacking.*

[Hijacking, skyjacking and carjacking are all a part of high risk life in the '90s, right? Well then, *sack-jacking* is sexual terrorism that deserves the same publicity and condemnation as these other heinous crimes.]

1. No.
2. I discovered that my last lover was bisexual.
3. My heart and I have this understanding.
4. I'm not into fireworks; I enjoy the 5th of July more than the 4th.
5. I'm not old enough.
6. I suffer from cold feet.
7. I'm climbing Mt. Rushmore in the morning.
8. My father is the west coast director of the N.R.A.
9. My last six kids were conceived using contraception.
10. No one can satisfy me like I can.
11. Masturbation is my greatest form of entertainment.
12. Sex makes me itch.
13. Sex makes me throw-up within 30-seconds of the act.
14. I'm a vegetarian.
15. I don't think I'd love you in the morning.
16. I don't think you'd love me after midnight.
17. My life is complicated enough as it is.
18. I have an appointment to get my hair done.

(continued on next page)

19. My baby brother is the leader of the Crips.
20. What was your name again?
21. Chocolate and semen don't mix.
22. Nice girls don't.
23. I'm practicing to become a nun.
24. I've got a virgin complex.
25. My kids will kill me.
26. I gain too much weight.
27. I'm allergic to sweat.
28. I'm allergic to sugar.
29. I don't want to ruin our friendship.
30. I don't have time to follow up.
31. I can't make love and breathe at the same time.
32. After I see current health certificates of the last 300 women you've slept with.
33. Have you seen "The Crying Game?"
34. Watch how I can pamper you with your pants on.
35. My lips are sealed.
36. I'm afraid I might incinerate.
37. I might not remember that I liked you.
38. I want to live to see the year 2000.
39. I can't afford the mortgage and a hospital bill.
40. I hate to eat and run.
41. I hate to eat on the run.
42. I pray over all of my sex partners first.

43. I'd just fall asleep.
44. It's never as much fun an it looks
    in the movies.
45. My pit bull is sensitive to loud noises.
46. I get nose bleeds.
47. I'm happier healthy.
48. I always call my mother first.
49. This is the second day of my 10-year
    moratorium on sex.
50. No, no, no, no, no.

---

CHAPTER 9

101 WAYS TO PAMPER YOUR BLACKMAN

ᗯ Now don't get overwhelmed. One-hundred-and-one of anything can be overwhelming. But you don't have to complete all 101 suggestions to pamper your man to his satisfaction. And *his* satisfaction, Ladies, is what we're talking about here.

Nothing on this *Pamper* list is frightfully expensive or even time-prohibitive. In fact, the best of these suggestions are free and take just minutes for you to perform. This is not like mental gymnastics—you don't even have to sweat. Just use your imagination and in no time you'll have him eating out of your hands!

1. Ask. Don't beg or demand.
2. Compliment him on his accomplishments.
3. Brag on him to your friends.
4. Prepare a candlelight dinner with all his favorite things.
5. Draw a scented candlelight bath for him (or for both of you).
6. Buy him flowers or a nice plant for his office.
7. Give him peace.

8. Organize his closet or sock drawer.
9. Keep yourself clean.
10. Surprise him with a manicure and pedicure.
11. Take his mother to lunch.
12. Buy him cologne or after shave.
13. Laugh with him; never at him.
14. Keep your bag of sexual tricks and treats full.
15. Be considerate of his idiosyncrasies.
16. Don't try to radically change him.
17. Be confident and self-sufficient.
18. Take him to a movie.
19. Cheer him on at his basketball games or in his bowling league.
20. Listen to him.
21. Tell him a story or read to him aloud.
22. Give him a massage.
23. Give him a foot massage.
24. Write love notes and hide them in his personal things.
25. Want the best for him.
26. Use your skills to help him plan his career and make his career moves.
27. Watch TV with him.
28. Don't gossip.
29. Have his favorite photo blown up and framed.
30. Clean his smudgy glasses with glass cleaner.
31. Buy him a new toothbrush when you notice the old one fraying.
32. Ask him to teach you something and take a real interest in learning it.

33. Encourage him.
34. Be sexy.
35. Be spontaneous and exciting.
36. Notice what's new about him.
37. Do an erotic striptease.
38. Learn to be a good cook.
39. Have meals ready on time.
40. Keep a clean, well stocked kitchen.
41. Wear perfume—on your body and in your hair.
42. Tell him a modern-day fairy tale in which he is the hero of the story.
43. Don't sulk.
44. Take him on a date.
45. Dance with him.
46. Don't remind him of his failures.
47. Love him for who he is.
48. Surprise him with his name on a removable tattoo in a secret place on your body.
49. Limit your time on the phone.
50. Apply a warm iron to his towel while he showers and sprinkle it with cologne. Have it waiting for him when he steps out of the shower.
51. Be polite.
52. Look at him when he's speaking.
53. Fix his coffee or tea and offer to bring it to him.
54. Cherish your time together.

55. Encourage him to stay within his budget and don't be the cause of his overspending.
56. Cut out articles from the newspaper he'll be interested in.
57. Call his mother to say hello.
58. Write him a thank you note.
59. Take him on a picnic.
60. Put the cap on the toothpaste.
61. Don't put his business in the streets.
62. Respect his privacy.
63. Allow him to have friends.
64. Don't snoop.
65. Buy him an x-rated magazine for the two of you to share.
66. Be faithful.
67. Respect him in front of your friends.
68. Give him a kiss for no reason.
69. Treat his ex-wife, the mother of his children, with respect.
70. Spend time with his kids.
71. Need and heed his advice.
72. Say what you mean and mean what you say.
73. Never share your secrets with anyone else.
74. Buy him a present for no reason.
75. Prepare a gourmet lunch for him to take to work.
76. Catalog his videocassettes.
77. Don't leave your hair in the bathroom wash basin.
78. Create a dessert and name it after him.

79. Check his shoes for shines and laces.
80. Take his clothes to the cleaners.
81. Never compare him to anyone.
82. Lip sync his favorite love song—
    with all the drama you can invent.
83. When you apologize, mean it.
84. Serve him breakfast in bed.
85. Keep a record of his special family
    commemorations— birthdays, graduations,
    anniversaries and deaths.
86. Stockpile a few greeting cards for him
    to use for his family remembrances.
87. Be his friend.
88. Don't nag or complain.
89. Encourage him to stay fit and healthy.
90. Learn how to tie his tie for him.
91. Encourage him to dream.
92. Even after you've won his heart,
    flirt with him.
93. Plant a tree in his honor.
94. Praise him to his children.
95. Make him "King for a Day."
96. Be mindful of his moods.
97. Save a few dollars each week for a
    surprise weekend get-away.
98. Be forgiving and don't hold grudges.
99. Make him a Christmas or
    Valentine's Day card.
100. Clean his comb and brush.
101. Pray for him and with him.

CHAPTER 10

THE KITCHEN IS OPEN
BUT THERE'S NO FREE LUNCH

∾ I don't care how much the Brother cares for you, Girlfriend, you can cancel yourself out of his life by pushing his credit to the limit. That Visa or American Express Gold card he's carrying is only plastic; not flesh and brawn.

The proof of a relationship is not the sum of its plastic parts. Shake him financially and he's sure to break you emotionally.

Now, he knows that you know caviar from catfish and veal from Vienna sausage, but what are you trying to prove by ordering the most expensive meal on the menu without any consideration of his budget?

[Forget his rent. His child support or car payment. Only the meal's for real in this deal.]

I have a friend who prides herself on how much it costs a gentleman to keep her entertained. She is on a first name basis with every maitre d' from New York to New Orleans. And not because *she's* picking up the tab.

The speculation is that this selfish Sister is a culinary courtesan, a gastronomic Mata Hari who won't leave a Brother with anything in his pocket but a toothpick.

❦   ❦   ❦

Another Sister—an attractive thirtysomething lady who couldn't tell you her Social Security number—takes pride in telling anyone who'll listen about her 100 pairs of shoes, who bought them, and how much he paid.

[This Sister is not a Clothes Horse. She is a Clothes Whore! Why, she barely wears the same outfit once.]

Her whole house, I'm told, is furnished in early African-American art—Tom, Dick and Malik.

[The pad must look like a museum of past relationships.]

❦   ❦   ❦

There are two types of women who almost never get their man: the Greedy Sister and the Needy Sister. Let me tell you, Girl, the kitchen is still open but they're not serving free lunch.

Wine and dine her, and the Greedy Sister will eat 'til she throws up. Her only focus is on how much she can get.

Now, when you take the Needy Sister to dinner, she'll finish her food, but she'll take home three more entrees in a doggy bag.

❦   ❦   ❦

I'll grant you that it's easy to be hungry for a little

pampering yourself in today's tight economy. It's awfully easy to be greedy if you're used to being needy.

And the average Sister today is needy. She is a single parent, trying to make ends meet with no help from the kids' father.

[Can I get a witness?]

Oh yes, most of us are needy.

Say you've got two kids in school. One needs braces; the other is in Little League. You're working two jobs trying to make it. Still you've got to sit on that old furniture. And you drive an old car that breaks down every other week. You haven't bought a new dress in three years.

Wouldn't it be nice, for a change, to have a man give you something besides a hard time? Treat you to a weekend in the woods? A shopping spree? Okay, a new pair of stockings that you don't have to pay for!

❦ ❦ ❦

I've got such a friend who was dating a swell Brother. He had a solid secure job, a little IRA and a decent life insurance policy. He wasn't rich, mind you, but he lived comfortably with his sister and her teenaged son.

My friend started seeing green after he spent one pleasant weekend in her well-appointed suburban Tudor-style home [that was her payoff in a costly divorce settlement].

She had the Brother fixing her leaky faucets, hanging pictures, and buying groceries and fertilizer for her exotic house plants.

The following weekend cost him a couple of CD's, a towel set and three bottles of imported water—in addition to taking her out two nights running.

Within the month, by her own estimate, the good Brother had spent over $1,000 on her, not counting his labor.

Nevertheless, the only cooking this Sister did was in the bedroom. She reckoned that he was not a guest in her home, but rather she was providing him weekend room and board.

This ill-advised Sister saw herself as saving him, not costing him. Sister-Girl obviously forgot that he didn't have to be there. The Brother had a place to lay his head and get his mail.

She was, in retelling how she had "gotten over," quite proud of the job she had worked on the man without him even knowing it.

A few months later she sadly reported that she and Brother-Man were no longer an item. Today, she is, I'm afraid, back to mowing her own lawn.

❦   ❦   ❦

Now, I'm not saying that every gesture of kindness a Brother makes has to be reciprocated. All I'm saying is that if you want to create a positive *himpression*, be considerate of his wallet, his time and the energy he is dedicating to your relationship.

Better to order the house wine and enjoy the blush

of your new romance than to demand a vintage French wine that will make his budget blush.

❦   ❦   ❦

Speaking of dinner, it's a good idea to show reciprocity, to take him out for dinner once in a while. Or, if your budget won't allow, cook for him every few dates. Men love a good home cooked meal. Especially perennial bachelors who have several restaurant menus committed to memory.

These guys are so microwave-friendly they even nuke the soup.

If you ask a Brother what he misses most about his mother, he'll usually say, *her cooking.*

[That should tell you something.]

❦   ❦   ❦

Now, a word about taking him out. It's not like you have to spend a fortune to prove that you care. You don't have to spring for tickets to an Anita Baker concert or a gourmet feast.

Every town has a fun joint, a little truck stop (frequently off the beaten track) that's loaded with color, atmosphere and low prices. [He *can't* pick anything on the menu that costs more than $5.95!]

Don't apologize for anything. Be just as proud of the $5.95 you spend on him as he is the $59.95 he's spent on you the night before.

[Girlfriend, please understand that you don't have to match him to catch him.]

While we're on the subject of pampering through the palate, don't forget, as the weather warms, that it is a perfect time for picnics.

You can plop your basket down virtually anywhere: in the park, the woods, at the beach or by the lake.

I once took a date on a picnic in a cemetery. Well, not just any cemetery. It was Forest Lawn Memorial Park—a bucolic setting in a sea of green lawn and trees, surrounded by squirrels, swans, and waterfalls.

After this out-of-this-world experience, I couldn't beat the brother off with a Ouija Board.

The point is you don't need to spend his last dime or yours to hold a Brother's interest.

❦   ❦   ❦

Listen, Girlfriend, you have to know how to play it.

Now, if the Brother makes a suggestion, it's perfectly alright to accept a gift. But if a shopping list comes from your lips, it may be one of the last requests you'll utter before he disappears into the aisles and gets himself lost in line.

If shopping is your turn-on, pamper him into thinking that it's his idea. Offer to cook him dinner and have him help you to shop for the things he likes.

In this way, if you sneak in a few goodies for yourself (like vitamins, bath salts or lotion) you won't look so greedy. Or needy. You won't *appear* to be desperate.

I totally blew that *appearance* thing one otherwise romantic evening when a gentleman friend offered to buy me flowers. I asked him instead if he'd take me to the drug store for a bottle of Vitamin C.

I didn't *need* flowers. I did *need* Vitamin C.

He agreed but was dismayed. We stopped dating a short time after this embarrassing incident.

❦   ❦   ❦

There's no telling how far you can throw a little subtlety.

Subtlety is what Brothers see in Southern girls. They know how to take an idea and make a man claim it as his own.

The same goes for Asian women, and yes, White women.

There, I've said it!

I've seen White women work their mojos on our Brothers without so much as working up a sweat. For many of them, pampering the Blackman is as easy as putting on a pair of pantyhose.

While many Sisters are throwing out evil looks and wild words to get what they want, ladies of other cultures are getting mileage out of a smile, a little encouragement, approval, recognition, a kiss hello or a kiss goodbye.

There's no telling how far a little kindness will go with our Brothers. If you have a problem giving anything more than a Brother requires, watch how some women can get an open line of credit in the bank of love, while other women have to pay to play and pay interest besides.

[Now who do you think is getting short-changed?]

Pampering the Blackman today is like the Red Cross serving the victims of Hurricane Andrew. There is always a point at which giving a little more makes more than a little difference.

CHAPTER 11

LOSS & THE LOVING VOID

People who try to hold on to their worldly goods in the face of a natural disaster usually become casualties of that disaster.

Like a very wealthy man I once knew who tried to cheat death by not writing a will. His only instruction was that he be buried beside his beloved mother in the family plot.

Well, when he died, his ex-wife and the children made sure that his body was cremated.

It just goes to show you.

The idea that we can hold on to material things is ridiculous.

The idea that we can hold on to a man is preposterous too.

Everything passes and everything must change.

Everything.

The past is where it belongs—behind us. If we use the experiences of the past to make us wiser, we learn to appreciate the joy of a moment without trying to squeeze eternity out of it.

Holding is not having.

No one belongs to us. You can squeeze the life out of a relationship or smother it to death by not allowing it to breathe.

All living things need air, water and room to grow.

Speaking of holding on, you can lose control of your relationship and spoil even the best thing with a trek through the painful pages of the past—his or yours.

You can't rewrite history. His story and your story—it's all history!

If I had a dollar for every woman I've met who has been hurt or lied to, I'd hold the keys to Las Vegas. The same applies to my good Brothers. We've all been down that road.

Further, in addition to being victims, most of us have been the victimizers.

Okay, not yesterday, maybe. But remember that super nice guy... the smart one who helped you with your freshman Algebra?

How many dates did you break with him after the football star hinted that he *might* be free Saturday night?

Hello!

Oh yes, we've all been the marksmen as well as the Incidental Target. [Remember "*Nice*"?]

Seasons of promiscuity, chronic negative behaviors, rages and cages—oh yes, we all carry old baggage. We all have memories.

So what else is new?

[Now, who's going to throw that first stone?]

It is amazing to me how much present time we dedicate to the past.

We're not going to spend any time on war stories here. They are just too gruesome. And far too repetitious.

All I want to say is, if you're living in the past, how on Earth, can you breathe in the present?

Enjoy the moment. Treasure the memory of a lost love and when it's over...

Well, that's coming up in the next chapter! Learn to turn the page.

The risk of loving is losing. For every victor there are a thousand losers.

You dis' one man and get your heart broken by the next five. That's life.

Let's face it—the odds are against all of us.

So why fall in love in the first place, when we can almost be certain that it will result in loss and pain?

Because if we try long enough, with all our hearts, we may win. Certainly over time the odds will improve and we will win enough victories to last a lifetime.

Love is always worth your trouble.

The most profound hurt I've experienced once brought me the most exquisite pleasure.

Drawing pleasure out of a memory of love is far richer than the mundane absence of it.

Can you count the times you've been in love? Okay, infatuated will do.

I've been infatuated hundreds of times and in love—I mean that hope-to-die love thing—over a dozen times. Each man, in his time, was the love of my life. And it was true. At that time.

When I look back through the years, I am grateful to each of my adored. For in giving my love, I received so much more.

One husband introduced me to the world of business. One lover gave me the gift of self-confidence. [I learned to stand up to him.]

Another Brother—who didn't stick around long enough to find out how much I cared for him—invited me to verbalize my ambition. He helped me to realize that I could accomplish anything.

In each case, with every man I have ever loved—in the long term—even the tears were well worth the investment.

Tears, it seems to me, are healthy expressions of loss. Wallowing in them, however, will drown you.

❦   ❦   ❦

The best way to get over an old hurt is to create a new situation for yourself. You only get stuck in the past when you constantly recreate it.

Speculation is pure recreation. The old *What If* game. What if he wasn't married? What if you had met him sooner? What if he'd met you later? What if he wasn't gay? What if his mother was dead? What if his father wasn't?

I know how you feel. We've all been down that bumpy road of speculation.

We get used to the pot holes and forget the damage its doing to our tires. In love, we get comfortable with the pain. It's familiar.

We seem to hold on to the horrors of lost loves like war medals—bringing them out of their gilded little boxes like trophies of misery.

And please don't think that perpetual heartache doesn't manifest itself in every aspect of your life either.

I see women everyday who are zombies of their own making, slaves to loss and rejection. They can't get over the pain. As a consequence, they can't get over. Behind the translucent veneer of chic togetherness is the stone-like facade of a woman scorned.

And you know what they say about a scorned woman. No man in his right mind buys a one-way ticket for a vacation in a rock quarry in Hell.

All I'm saying, Girlfriend, is that everyone has a past. But no one is doomed to repeat it in perpetuity. This is not "The Twilight Zone."

The price you pay for loving deeply is hurting much. But don't let that hurt shut down your emotional generator. The only way you can accept a new love is to let go of the old hurts.

I used to always be in love with a man. I was a magnet for love. My love life was like a trapeze artist—swinging from one relationship to another, with a few seconds of suspended hurt in between.

When you are falling out of love, I've found that there is usually a *Loving Void*. A *Loving Void* is the space between the old relationship you are leaving and the new one you have yet to discover.

You know, like cleaning out your garage. There is always an emptiness that accompanies clearing out the old junk in your life.

It's tempting to fill the *Loving Void* with the first man who rings your bell. [Like buying up everything you see at the first garage sale you come across.]

Please resist the temptation. You're not ready for anything except healing.

To heal yourself, to prepare for the healthy relationship you truly deserve, you've got to go to work.

I believe in self-help—anything you can do to get better.

Take a class, get active in a sport or exercise program, try a new look, haircut, move, decorate. Develop an interest outside of your problems. Help the homeless. Join a church or a civic group.

Do something positive for yourself and for others.

You'll be so busy, so entertained, and so proud of yourself that you'll hardly notice time passing.

Staying busy, filling your time with nurturing activities will naturally make you a more interesting person and a more attractive person to be around.

Learn to appreciate your loss and the *Loving Void* like the silence in a still night. Find peace in the void.

Some time ago I wrote a little thank you poem to a man with whom I was destined to share only one wonderful weekend. I hope it puts this *loss* thing in a little clearer perspective.

People come,
Some stay,
Some pass.
Not everything is made to last.
Sometimes the best
Is just a little treat.
It doesn't hang around long
But it sure is sweet.

CHAPTER 12

GOODBYE... GOODBYE... GOODBYE AGAIN: WHEN IT'S TIME TO LEAVE

꙾ I don't care how great it was between you, when it's over, it's over. Learn to love generously and leave graciously.

I had a friend who loved a certain Brother more than a baby loves milk. The problem was, the feeling wasn't mutual.

The Sister finally nagged her way into a wedding band but, almost before the honeymoon sheets were changed, the Brother was asking for a divorce.

During one final moment of passion she poked a hole in her diaphragm. Lo and behold the Sister became pregnant.

Quietly accepting his fate, the Brother stopped asking for a divorce. As a matter of fact, he stopped everything—sex, dinner, coming home for days at a time.

Less than a year after their daughter's birth, it came as no surprise to anyone when he announced that he was moving out.

Unable to work, my now emotional-wreck-of-a-friend spent her days and nights plotting against her "ex" and hating his gorgeous slender new girlfriend.

Hate, in fact, ate her alive. Soon the Brother stopped visiting her altogether; meeting his daughter, instead, at the home of his former mother-in-law.

That, of course, made the Sister hate the Brother all the more. Her rage resulted in a nervous breakdown.

In and out of mental institutions for the past 10 years, this once-attractive Sister looks 20 years older than she really is and no one wants her.

Today, the Brother and his pretty young wife have custody of his child. They live in a beautiful house in suburban Los Angeles, with his daughter and a son of their own.

Life goes on!

Another friend spent her years plotting how to get her man back into her arms. She could not accept his claim of no longer loving her.

Eight years later, on his wedding day to a woman he'd known for less than a month, he still didn't love my friend.

Just imagine the positive, self-enhancing things she could have done with those eight years.

She could have gone through medical school with all the energy she'd invested into getting her ex-boyfriend back into her arms.

I think of a failed love affair as a meal. Yesterday's lunch is today's bowel movement. That doesn't mean that it wasn't good; it's just over. [Flush!]

꽃   꽃   꽃

The best you can do, my Sisters, is maintain your dignity when it's time to part. Let him remember you as a lady.

Having been in this position too many times to count, I can tell you, groveling makes you hate yourself and him too. You, for doing it, him for witnessing it.

Besides, who are you mad at anyway? Him, for leaving? Or yourself, for ignoring the signs?

Think about it.

There were signs, of course. There are always signs.

Where once he hung on your every word, now he hangs you by your words.

Remember when he called you five times a day? Now you call him once and he's busy.

At the height of your romance he always bought tickets for two. Now he needs his space.

Now the only flowers, love notes and wine labels you have are the ones pressed into your book of memories.

He is bored. He is glum. He is passive. He is aggressive. He is sad. Angry. Irritable. Distracted. He is gaining weight or he's losing his temper. He's absent-minded, he's late or he's gone.

Girlfriend, if your Brother-Man is tired, maybe he's just tired of you!

I don't need to tell you, dear Sister, you may not know where he is coming from, but you know that he's going.

You may not know where he's going but you know that his heart is already out the door.

❦   ❦   ❦

So what are you going to do about it? You've lost your grip as you watch the lustre of love slip into a state of rust.

Some sad Sisters opt for revenge. Revenge, they say, is sweet.

But the thrill of getting even lasts no longer than the thrill of taking a plunge off a 50-foot cliff. It is a cheap thrill that causes a lot of damage.

Causing him misery or getting even, is certain emotional suicide for you too. If he didn't care for you before; your reviling acts of terrorism, subterfuge and sabotage will only brand you as a malcontent or lunatic in his mind.

This is a tough one, my Sisters. And many of you will argue that I've missed the mark. You *have to* make him pay for the shabby way he treated you.

But let's look at the short and the long terms of your cheap thrill.

What's the Brother going to think about you when the door slams shut? And what will you think of yourself, say, in ten years or so, when you bump into him on the street? Or you are reintroduced at a party?

A certain Sister I know planned revenge on her former boyfriend down to the microscopic detail. She kept a list of revolting acts in a little journal she liked to show her friends.

I remember only a few of her pranks: sugar in his gas tank, rotten eggs thrown against his house, telegrams charged to his telephone and a number of midnight calls to disturb his sleep.

Twenty years later, I was told, she had to face that same Brother over a desk. Unwittingly she had applied for a job for which she was imminently qualified. Her former boyfriend was the newly hired vice president of Personnel.

Life certainly offers interesting little twists, doesn't it?

In this case, the Sister made her own noose and then hung herself with it 20 years later.

❦   ❦   ❦

Now after marriage and divorce, a few engagements and a hundred relationships—of greater or lesser degrees of intimacy—I've finally learned that *Goodbye* is a beautiful word.

If only we could take *Goodbye*, like art, at face value, instead of trying to rework it to fit our egos.

Sisters today don't understand the lengths a Brother will go to get away, if he wants to leave.

He will run, hide, move, change his name, anything to make tracks away from a Sister he no longer wants to be bothered with. [Ouch!]

You can pout. You can stomp. You can cry or faint. You can threaten. You can beg. You can burn his clothes or call Nigeria from his telephone. When the Brother wants to get his hat, he's history.

Just ask any Brother. There are more than 50 ways to leave your lover.

Well, if there is nothing you can do to get him back why not just let him go?

The least you can do—with words or in silence—is maintain your dignity. Don't get caught up in the emotions of the moment.

Sometimes you just can't keep quiet. You've got to speak the words. You need to explain why it's time for you to part.

Now if you can't seem to get the words out—because there's too much pain or too much emotion behind them, how about a loving letter? A telephone call?

It's your play but don't let that be your excuse for bad behavior. Your last great act of pampering the Brother should be to leave your positive prints on his memory.

Okay, so you flubbed the last one. You don't have to repeat all your errors, do you?

I know several Sisters who maintain close friendly relationships with a number of their ex-boyfriends.

They can ask a favor, get an escort or make a new

business buddy out of their former lovers with ease.

The door, for these smart Sisters, is always open because they didn't break the man's arm off when the door was closing.

They have the uncanny ability to turn sour grapes into sweet wine.

For them the simple philosophy is: the greater the differences, the greater the opportunity for compromise. They won't be done in by a break up.

I watched one Sister go through such a difficult parting with a man who said he no longer cared for her.

She had assumed that their three-month-old relationship had a future. She was committed. He was committed only to play the field after he hit a home run.

I watched her go through the stages: she was dismayed—stunned—shocked. She was so hurt that she became angry at herself for her naiveté. In one week, however, she waxed philosophical.

"You know, since he doesn't like me," she said one day, "it was really kind of him to let me get on with my life."

And that's exactly what she did, with a smile.

The Brother was so shocked by her reaction he couldn't leave her alone. They became the best of friends. Finally this good Brother came to his senses and realized that he had the pick of the pack. Today they are married, expecting their first child.

Of course most romances don't have such tight storybook endings.

I have another friend who has this philosophy, which she shares with each new love interest: "I may be easy to leave but I'm hard to forget."

This lady confesses that most of the men she's been close to can't get used to being treated well. She admits that almost every Brother she's been with has left her for a cute, clinging, nagging and possessive little shrew in sheep's clothing.

As the romance wears thin, she simply steps aside.

The amazing thing is that they all come back. Only then do they remember her words. When she turns the page [on a relationship] she also closes the book.

This Sister is proud to say that she is on friendly terms with all of her former boyfriends.

ξ   ξ   ξ

Now, I'll admit, my Sister, that men don't necessarily play by our rules. Maybe he dogged you. Maybe he stole your money. Maybe he forgot to mention that he's married.

The point is, you did get something out of it, didn't you?

[If only a good lesson, you did get something.]

In the '90s era of fierce competition, you've got to throw out that old rule book. Today the play is to either wallow in self-pity or dust off your ego and get back out on the field. Those, dear Sister, are often the only two choices you have.

Life goes on. It really does.

If you really want to get the knack of pampering the Blackman, learn to recognize a once sweet song turning into a broken record.

When the music stops, there is only one sensible thing to do. Don't forget the tune but turn off the radio and preserve your batteries.

The fact is, Girlfriend, that we are all living in the fast lane. In any relationship, you don't have to go the distance together to enjoy the ride.

In conclusion...

Now, you know that's a lie. *Himpressions: The Blackwoman's Guide To Pampering The Blackman* is only the first installment of my thoughts on Black relationships—as a Blackwoman, writer, and the single parent of a manchild.

The truth is, I'm just getting warmed up.

Like talking on the phone to a friend you haven't spoken to in five years, you want to stay up all night playing "catch up."

Credential wise, I'm just another Blackwoman. Although my training and background in communications qualifies me to comment on relationships from a social science point of view, my propositions are based on sense, not science. It is the sense we all have but too infrequently use. Common sense has become, all too often, quite uncommon.

Certainly we all have a lot to say about the troubled state of Black male-female relationships. It is my great hope that this *Guide* inspires people to say what's on their minds. The time for silence is past.

It doesn't much matter if you approve/disapprove or like/dislike this writer's *himpressions*. I hope, in fact, that you'll pick my ideas apart like a piece of meat stuck between your teeth.

It will make me happy if you just think about them. And if anything I have to say works for another Sister or helps a relationship to survive in these chaotic times, then my *himpressions* have been worth sharing.

In keeping with the brevity of this manual, and in hopes that a Sister can glean just one idea that will enhance her relationship with a Brother, I've condensed the essence of my *himpressions* into a pocket-size list of 20 Do's and Don'ts. I call them *Himpression Nuggets.*

Although they've all been said a thousand times before in a thousand different ways—like *I love you* in a song. You can listen and listen but you can't hear it enough.

The truth is, you could possibly condense this entire book into a three-panel cartoon, a song or a painting. It could take on any form. But I'm a writer; not a cartoonist, songwriter or artist.

So here we go, *Himpressions* in a nutshell or...

Do...

1. Be inventive, cleaver and creative.
   Do the thoughtful things that require your
   imagination.

2. Bend like a tree in matters of preference.
   But be hard as a rock in matters of principle.

3. Smile. Laugh. Remember, sunshine
   can even melt snow.

4. Be yourself—inside and out, get clean
   and natural. Save the $30 you were going to
   spend on acrylic fingernails for a dinner
   out or a gift of love.

5. Clean up your act; clean up your flat.
   He may live like a pig but your home should
   be a refuge from his sty.

6. Cherish every moment of your time together. Become a time ecologist—don't waste it arguing, harboring jealousy or trying to manipulate the moment.

7. Want the best for him. If you are the best, what a team you'll make! If you're not, find a new field to play in.

8. Unless you have happy, secure and caring friends and family, leave your business at home. Remember, misery always loves to meddle.

9. Help! The Blackman needs help in the '90s as never before. We all do. Discarded, damaged and skeptical, we are waging war against each other on economic, psychological and spiritual fronts. You can assist in healing by helping.

10. Hold the relationship in the same esteem you hold your job. The same etiquette applies: show up on time, do your share of the work and make a positive contribution to the team.

11. Take the stuff so seriously. Be serious about one thing; being happy. In the Bible, this is reinforced in Proverbs 15:15. "A cheerful heart has a continual feast." There will always be *stuff,* and a lot of it; like sickness, the loss of a job, the weather. Some things you just can't control. Learn to roll with the waves of change and you'll be a survivor on the sea of life.

12. Carry old baggage into your new hotel suite. His-story, her-story, it's all history.

13. Be selfish. Now, self-first is not being selfish but if you insist on being Queen of the Me's, be prepared to reign over an empty court.

14. Count on perfection. Lord knows, you're not perfect. Remember everything in nature is flawed, including nature's grandest master-pieces. To the cynical, the Grand Canyon is just a bunch of jagged rocks. Imperfection is another word for individuality.

15. Judge the horse by its saddle. Many wonderful catches drive a bus, deliver mail or dig ditches. Take a few turns around the corral and you may be surprised to learn that the quiet, Toyota-driving cowboy over there belongs to a credit union, has great health benefits and, quite often, does a little hustle on the side. He may do landscaping on the weekends, real estate during off hours or tax preparation during the season.

16. Nag. Oh yeah, add whine to this one. Especially at inappropriate times. For one thing, a whining, nagging woman is sure to be ignored. Men hate it. By the way, never, never call him on the job with a complaint. It may be your dime but what can he do on the boss's time?

17. Put sex first. You may be good, Sister, but to hold a man's attention these days, you better have more rap than just in the bedroom.

18. Rush the bloom of a fresh romance. Savor every step of its unfoldment. Like a good stew, the longer it simmers, the better it will taste.

19. Expect to get your size-eight feet into a size-six shoe. If the shoes don't fit, get yourself another pair that do. Not every relationship is 'til death do you part.

20. Lose your upper hand by taking your fortune for granted. If you are blessed with a man who loves and respects you, you are holding an Ace. When you treat him like a King you are his Queen. With the three most powerful trump cards in the deck, the only way you can lose is to throw away your hand.

HIMPRESSIONS ORDER FORM

☐ Please put me on your mailing list for the upcoming *Himpressions* quality line of tee shirts, sports caps and coffee mugs.

☐ Please send me information on *Himpressions* workshops and seminars.

Name:

Address:

City, State and Zip Code:

Total Amount Enclosed:

Mail To: Turn The Page Productions
1147 E. Broadway, Suite #121, Glendale, CA 91205

HIMPRESSIONS ORDER FORM

☐ Please put me on your mailing list for the upcoming
Himpressions quality line of tee shirts, sports caps and
coffee mugs.

☐ Please send me information on *Himpressions* workshops
and seminars.

Name:

Address:

City, State and Zip Code:

Total Amount Enclosed:

Mail To: Turn The Page Productions
1147 E. Broadway, Suite #121, Glendale, CA 91205

HIMPRESSIONS ORDER FORM

☐ Please put me on your mailing list for the upcoming
Himpressions quality line of tee shirts, sports caps and
coffee mugs.

☐ Please send me information on *Himpressions* workshops
and seminars.

Name:

Address:

City, State and Zip Code:

Total Amount Enclosed:

Mail To: Turn The Page Productions
1147 E. Broadway, Suite #121, Glendale, CA 91205